THE *ABC's*

OF RELATIONSHIPS

*a guide to understanding and
building great relationships*

MARION MEYERS

DESTINY IMAGE™ EUROPE srl
Via Maiella, 1
66020 San Giovanni Teatino (Ch) – Italy

"Changing the world, one book at a time."

This book and all other Destiny Image™ Europe books are available at Christian bookstores and distributors worldwide.

To order products, or for any other correspondence:

DESTINY IMAGE™ EUROPE srl
Via Acquacorrente, 6
65123 - Pescara - Italy
Tel. +39 085 4716623 - Fax: +39 085 9431270
E-mail: info@eurodestinyimage.com
Or reach us on the Internet: www.eurodestinyimage.com

ISBN: 978-88-96727-05-8
For Worldwide Distribution, Printed in the U.S.A.
1 2 3 4 5 6 7 8 / 14 13 12 11 10

Acknowledgments

One Sunday in church, while holding the man-hand of my now grown-up son, I thought how blessed I am to have had three generations of men hold my hand throughout my life. First, my dad. Thank you, Dad, for holding my hand and loving me *all* the days of my life. You still add so much to me, and I thank God for giving me a dad just like you. Second, my husband. God could not have chosen a better life partner to hold my hand these past 25 years. Once again, thank you, Honey, for all your support and encouragement; you certainly are my cheerleader. Third, my son. I have been so delighted to hold your hand, my boy, and I thank God for how you now hold mine. You are truly growing into a wonderful man of God.

My beloved mom, I love you; and whenever we are not together, I miss you so very much.

My daughter, you are my princess, my joy, and my reward. I love you always and know we will enjoy many exciting journeys together.

My friend Diana, I am so grateful to God for the gift you are to me. Thank you for every way you have blessed my life.

My WIT ladies, I cannot imagine a world without you. Thank you for your never-ending love and support. Together we will do *whatever it takes* to make Jesus famous and to make a difference to those God connects us with.

Endorsements

This pivotal book is as practical as it is powerful. Forged from personal and pastoral experience, this well-researched and readable publication marries incisive analysis to solid implementation. Marion Meyers is a gifted teacher and communicator and also a very dear friend. We heartily commend her latest book to you.

John Glass, General Superintendent,
Elim Pentecostal Churches
Marilyn Glass, Founder of Aspire,
Elim's national women's initiative

Marion Meyers has the rare ability to bring clarity and understanding to a dimension of life that many of us find difficult to navigate—relationships. Marion's clear and easy-to-read style makes this book a must-have resource to enrich our lives and the lives of those with whom we have relationships.

Arianna Walker
Executive Director
Mercy Ministries, UK

Table of Contents

———————

Foreword

We have known Marion and Michael Meyers for about 25 years. They lived in our home for six months in 1986 and even though, since then, we have lived in different cities on different continents, through the years we have stayed in touch and maintained our friendship.

Many relationships never go beyond the surface and others come and go, but the ones that endure become more precious through the years. The older we get, the more we understand that our relationships and connections with each other are more important than anything else in our lives; and it stands to reason that we should always be open to learn better communication skills and to continue to grow in this area.

Marion is a godly woman and a wonderful wife, mother, pastor, and friend. She is a caring, giving person and a joy to know. She is personally submitted to the Word of God and to the Holy Spirit; she leads by example. We have watched her grow in the Lord through the years and have seen the sweet fruit of her life mature. Even though Marion has faced many challenges—as we all do—we have seen her face them, work through them, and emerge better and stronger.

Proverbs 4:23 says, "Keep your heart with all diligence, for out of it spring the issues of life." Your relationships are everything, and everything hinges on your attitude toward them! Marion's first book, *The ABC's of Emotions*, was a great blessing to us personally and touched countless people around the world. Your emotions affect everything in your life, especially your relationships.

In this new book, Marion deals with our relationships specifically in the areas of self, God, and others. We know that *The ABC's of Relationships* is going to be a great help and blessing to you. As you read it, receive it and apply it to your life; we believe you will see wonderful, positive results!

Drs. Rodney and Adonica Howard-Browne
Tampa, Florida, USA

Preface

There are many things in our lives that are optional, but relationships are not one of them. From the time of our conception until the time of our death, we will be involved in relationships, and the only choice we have is to build them up or tear them down. As we are God's own handiwork and have been created in His image and likeness for the purpose of relationship, so we carry around with us a deep need and longing for meaningful relationships. Our God is a relational God and His plan for us is to enjoy rich, satisfying, and fulfilling relationships where we both receive and give great joy to those we do life with.

Relationship is simply defined as a "connection, association, or involvement with others." When we have no or too-little connectedness or have experienced painful relationships, then we experience this as misery and trauma. Most of our pain, if not all of it, is experienced emotionally—like rejection, failure, anger, bitterness, stress, loneliness, anxiety, grief, guilt, and is caused by the breakdown of essential or meaningful relationships in our lives. The ability to resolve conflict and develop the necessary skills for satisfying, healthy, and fulfilling relationships plays an enormous role in our success and happiness in this life.

God's Word, the Bible, is still the best handbook ever written on human behavior. In the Bible, I discovered that there are three types of relationships. First, we have a connection to our Creator and heavenly Father, which is neither complicated nor difficult, especially when we understand the loving heart of God. Second, we relate and associate with ourselves, which tends to be a lot more complex, as we can dislike ourselves, get disappointed or angry with ourselves, or take pride in ourselves. Third, we have relationship with other people. This can be a minefield fraught with difficulty because relating to others successfully can be confusing and discouraging, or at other times, fulfilling and exhilarating.

In the greatest commandment ever given to humankind, we are instructed, or rather commanded, to have a loving and caring connection with all three types of relationships.

> *Jesus answered him, "The first of all the commandments is: 'Hear, O Israel, the Lord our God, the Lord is one. And **you shall love the Lord your God** with all your heart, with all your soul, with all your mind, and with all your strength.' This is the first commandment. And the second, like it, is this: '**You shall love your neighbor as yourself.**' There is no other commandment greater than these"* (Mark 12:29-31).

In this my second book, I cover 26 different issues, skills, and dynamics of all three types of relationships. The qualities and skills needed to have these relationships are all found in His Word. God would not command us if He did not first give us all the tools to accomplish the task. With God's Word, I share these tools with you, and with a disciplined and determined effort, I am sure that every child of God can make life-changing progress.

When I started a whole new program at the gym, I got a whole new revelation about pain. My trainer's motto was "there can be no gain without pain!" At times I could barely walk up the stairs to the changing rooms, but I was happy to do it "for the joy set before me," which was a fitter, healthier me. All of us can make choices to bring healing and wholeness to our lives by enhancing our relationships.

As with my first book, *The ABC's of Emotions*, this book is an A-Z multivitamin catalog for relationships. You can read all 26 chapters in order, or you can just dip in and out of the chapters that may be the most meaningful to you. My heartfelt prayer is that every chapter you read will touch your life in some way and make you more emotionally whole so that you enjoy healthier and more fulfilling relationships. It is by no means exhaustive in its scope, as no book can be. May it arouse in you hunger like never before to pursue the peace that is rightfully yours.

> *Let him turn away from wickedness and shun it, and let him do right. Let him search for peace (harmony; undisturbedness from fears, agitating passions, and moral conflicts) and seek it eagerly. [Do not merely desire peaceful relations with God, with your fellowmen, and with yourself, but pursue, go after them!]"* (1 Peter 3:11 AMP).

Chapter 1

Altering Attitudes

INTRODUCTION

Many different aspects and issues are going to be explored over the next 26 chapters, but the first one will set a foundation upon which all the others will be built. Viktor Frankl, survivor of the Nazi concentration camp, said "Everything can be taken from a man but the last of the human freedoms—to choose one's attitude in any given set of circumstances"[1]. Romans 12:2 promises us the change that as new creatures in Christ we long to experience. The Amplified Version of this Scripture helps us understand that this transformation involves the entire renewal of our minds, including our attitudes.

> Do not be conformed to this world (this age), [fashioned after and adapted to its external, superficial customs], but be transformed (changed) by the [entire] renewal of your mind [by its new ideals *and its new attitude*], so that you may prove [for yourselves] what is the good and acceptable and perfect will of God, even the thing which is good and acceptable and perfect [in His sight for you] (Romans 12:2 AMP).

THE IMPORTANCE OF ATTITUDE

One definition of *attitude* is an inward feeling expressed by behavior. The Oxford Dictionary also breaks it down into two areas: a settled way of thinking or feeling, and a posture of the body. In other words, you *wear* an attitude—it's not only inward and hidden, but it manifests outwardly in all that you do and say, whether you are aware of it or not. Synonyms of attitude are demeanor, disposition, inclination, mental state, mindset, mood, opinion, perspective, position, prejudice, reaction, standpoint, and view.

From this definition, we begin to understand why it is so important to have our attitudes aligned with the Word of God. John Maxwell, in his book *The Winning Attitude*, states, "Our attitude is the primary force that will determine whether we succeed or fail."[2] The bottom line is that our attitudes will many times make or break us because they make decisions for us that we might not even consciously be aware of. Our attitude might decide before we even have a chance to get to know someone that we are not going to like them. Our attitude might decide for us whether we will cope well and maturely with relational difficulties before we are even in the midst of them. Our attitudes determine how we handle life, deal with our failures, and manage our relationships. Ultimately, our attitudes can determine the quality of our lives, and as Dr. Edwin Louis Cole says, "Attitude determines the altitude of life."[3]

Our pastor when we lived in South Africa often said, "When the toothpaste tube is squeezed, then we will see what comes out!" I have found that God has allowed many a trial or test into my life in order to squeeze my toothpaste tube and show me just how bad my attitude is. The test will reveal to us and others how spiritual we really are—either we will practice the love-walk we say we believe in and become doers of the Word, or we will allow the flesh to have its way and react with complaining, bitterness, anger, and negativity. "For this was my purpose in writing you, to **test your attitude** and see if you would stand the test, whether you are obedient and altogether agreeable [to following my orders] in everything" (2 Cor. 2:9 AMP). After many a fleshly moment I would hear the still small voice of the Holy Spirit discipline me simply with the words "Fail!" Everyday life tests your attitude. These unguarded times are when God gives us the precious insight and discernment as to who we really are!

As a pastor, I once had to admonish a young leader in this area of her life; for although she was naturally blessed with gifting and intelligence, her attitude was a consistent problem. As the above definition describes, this person's demeanor and default perspective, reaction, mood, and view were always negative. Many of her church co-workers used to joke that her bad attitude would arrive in the building before she did. Such an attitude was truly a failing that was sabotaging not only her relationships but also her destiny in God. It is important for us to understand that our attitude is very influential as it goes out ahead of us and meets people long before we have even shown up!

As self-insight is always the doorway to our deliverance, and as we need to know what our problems are before we can begin to overcome them, we need to be quick to first examine our own attitudes. This can be simply done by asking yourself some direct questions, such as "How do I feel life is treating me?" or "Is my cup always half empty or half full?" Listen to what is coming out of your mouth because the words you speak will always give you away. The Book of Luke tells us "for out of the abundance of the heart his mouth speaks" (Luke 6:45).

John Maxwell concludes, "If your attitude toward the world is excellent, you will receive excellent results. If you feel so-so about the world, your response from the world will be average. Feel badly about your world, and you will seem only to have negative feedback from life."[4] This is a spiritual principle that is taught to us in Galatians 6:7: "Whatever a man sows, this he will also reap." Therefore, whatever attitude and corresponding action that you have in your relationships is what will produce the outcome of your life.

WHAT SHOULD OUR ATTITUDE BE IN OUR RELATIONSHIP?

> *Let this mind* [attitude, purpose, view, opinion, disposition] *be in you which was also in Christ Jesus, who, being in the form of God, did not consider it robbery to be equal with God, but made Himself of no reputation, taking the form of a bondservant, and coming in the likeness of men. And being found in appearance as a man, He humbled Himself and became obedient to the point of death, even the death of the cross"* (Philippians 2:5-8).

This Scripture instructs us as to what our attitude should be patterned upon; it is the one underlying principle that we should adhere to in all our relationships. This key to our success lies in how Christ responded to those around Him. We are instructed to be imitators of Christ and our attitude needs to be a copy of the original.

God is not requiring us to die on a cross as Jesus did, but He is expecting us to crucify the flesh on a daily basis. The only Christian mandate we have been given is to be Christ-like in all our relationships. How quickly I like to forget the preceding verses in Philippians 2:3-4: "Let nothing be done through selfish ambition or conceit, but in lowliness of mind let each esteem others better than himself. Let each of you look out not only for his own interests, but also for the interests of others." Jesus humbled Himself so completely, setting for us the ultimate example of humility, and we can only conclude that humility must be the underlying attitude of all our relationships. Let me add an important footnote here, as I have previously counseled several people with this possible confusion. At no time and in no way does the above mandate contradict the healthy stewardship of self that God requires from us. Healthy stewardship of self includes practicing assertiveness and boundary setting, and I speak about these in consequent chapters. Self-definition is not in any way to be confused with selfishness or a lack of humility.

Humility includes a tender heart toward God that is teachable and pliable. Many of us might feel we fulfill this requirement, but we will also admit that at the same time we struggle to fulfill His Word in relation to those around us. Let's read what First John 4:20 says about this: "If someone says, 'I love God,' and hates his brother, he is a liar; for he who does not love his brother whom he has seen, how can he love God whom he has not seen?" Andrew Murray, in his book *Humility*, says, "We cannot possibly have true humility as we approach the Father in our relationship with Him, as we talk and walk with Him, if we are not walking in humility with those around us. Humility before God can only be proved to be real in our behavior toward others. In fact our whole relationship with God can only proved to be real when we live it out in front of other people."[5] "Live in harmony with one another; do not be haughty (snobbish, high-minded, exclusive), but readily adjust yourself to [people, things] and give yourselves to humble tasks. Never overestimate yourself or be wise in your own conceits" (Rom. 12:16 AMP).

How Do We Change?

For the children of God, change is inevitable and integral to their walk with Jesus; we are forever changing, becoming more and more like Him. In Matthew 7:12, Jesus gives us one golden rule that should govern all our actions toward others: "Therefore, whatever you want men to do to you, do also to them." Here are five easy-to-remember vowels to help you remember how to act and respond in all your relationships:

- **A** is for *Appreciate*. Adopt an attitude of appreciation. If you want to be appreciated, make it a daily habit to appreciate, value, affirm, and thank others. One of the deepest needs in human nature is to be appreciated. Whenever you meet someone, within the first 30 seconds of conversation, try to say something that shows you appreciate them. It will set the tone for the rest of your time together as it will give them a sense of worth to you. If you had to start treating people as really important to you, they will soon start treating you the same. Most of us think wonderful things about people, but they never know it as we are too stingy with our praise. Your thoughts are of no value if you just think them and don't share them.

- E is for *Encourage*: Appreciate who they are and encourage what they do. We avoid people who put us down and seek out those who believe in us and lift us up. Our close friends are those who encourage us. Serving others and investing in them is not demeaning but fulfilling and rewarding. Likewise, the unhappiest people are those who wonder how the world is going to make them happy. If you are always looking to others to make you happy then you will stay the victim. "Love one another with brotherly affection [as members of one family], giving precedence and showing honor to one another" (Rom. 12:10 AMP).

- I is for *Incline* your ear. There is a difference between hearing people and really listening to them; listening is wanting to hear and being interested in what is being said. If you are the type of person who arrives in a room and says "here I am" rather than "there you are," you will always be self-focused and showing honor only to yourself. Listening attentively and carefully and intelligently to others will give them a sense of value. Form a habit of showing an interest in the details of other people's lives.

- O is for *Overlook* the Offense.

    Therefore, as the elect of God, holy and beloved, put on tender mercies, kindness, humility, meekness, longsuffering; bearing with one another, and forgiving one another, if anyone has a complaint against another; even as Christ forgave you, so you also must do (Colossians 3:12-13).

Pride is often the biggest stumbling block to releasing forgiveness. If you want others to forgive you and take into account your intentions as well as your behavior, then be quick to forgive. We all have a deep desire for total forgiveness. A forgiving spirit is one of the basic and necessary ingredients for a healthy relationship. Forgiveness frees us from guilt and allows us to interact positively with other people.

- U is for *Understanding.* Understanding is a vital ingredient to good communication, which is essential to a healthy relationship. Don't be so arrogant that you think you know it all. Do not presume you understand—everyone wants to be understood properly, so strive to understand where people are coming from and what their intentions are, not just their outward behavior. How badly does it hurt and stress you when you feel misunderstood?

If you start obeying His Word by appreciating, encouraging, inclining your ear to, overlooking the offenses of, and understanding others, you truly will have the same mind (attitude) as was in Christ Jesus (see Phil. 2:5). Start sowing today those things that you would love to reap in your own life.

ENDNOTES

1. Viktor E. Frankl, *Man's Search for Meaning* (New York, NY: Washington Square Press, Simon and Schuster, 1963), 104.

2. John Maxwell, *The Winning Attitude* (Nashville, TN: Thomas Nelson Publishers, 1993), 26.

3. http://www.brainyquote.com/quotes/quotes/e/edwin-louis360075.html.

4. John Maxwell, *The Winning Attitude* (Nashville, TN: Thomas Nelson Publishers, 1993), 27.

5. Andrew Murray, *Humility* (Alachua, FL: Bridge-Logos Publishers, 2000), 41 paraphrased.

Chapter 2

Building Better Boundaries

Good fences make good neighbors.

–Robert Frost

INTRODUCTION

The law of gravity comes into play whether we understand, ac-knowledge, or agree with it, and so do boundaries. Boundaries help de-fine us and can have a major influence on our relationships with both God and man. They are one of the greatest pillars of any relationship, and I will be bold enough to say that no healthy relationship can be built without boundaries in place and enforced.

The definition of a *boundary* is "something that indicates a border or limit."[1] In the natural world, it indicates the borders of a property and refers to what someone owns and is responsible for. Some country bor-ders have very little markings or indication, making it difficult to know if you have crossed over from one country to the next. Others have mas-sive security and protection in place. A core principle of boundaries is that of protection, keeping anything at bay that is not good.

This kind of boundary mark or definition, however, does not affect our lives half as much as an emotional boundary. An emotional bound-ary may be invisible but it can be very clearly defined and largely deter-mines who you are in relation to others, and vice versa. It also allocates clear limits and expectations of responsibility. Your boundaries should protect your treasures, those riches and resources that you possess, both internally and externally, which are essential and precious to your own life. Just as an owner of real estate may be angry when someone trespasses on his land, so we may become angry and upset when another person trespasses over our personal boundary markings and into our private land, taking our treasures.

If we do not know where the boundaries are, we cannot respect others' boundaries and cannot enforce our own. This is often the reason for many of the destructive and dysfunctional relationships that plague our lives. Depression, codependency, anxiety, and many other conditions can improve by becoming aware of and enforcing our personal boundaries. Unfortunately, this core principle of relationships is never explained or taught to us while we are growing up, and many of us must discover these truths through the costly experience of broken relationships. The Word says to "train up a child in the way that he should go, and when he is old he will not depart from it" (Prov. 22:6). This is true in the positive and the negative. We get taught, consciously and subconsciously, some negative relational skills that we then keep until we are old.

Today is a good time to question what we have been taught and allow these things to be held up to the light of God's Word. God wants us to know why we are hurting and how to heal. "Behold, You desire truth in the inward parts, and in the hidden part You will make me to know wisdom" (Ps. 51:6). I pray that the truth of God's Word in this chapter will set you free.

The adult in you now must take charge of your re-education and instruct the child within you. Remember that boundaries teach us that we are primarily responsible for "us," which is the biblical stewardship of self. The truth that we find as adults must set us free from the old painful and childish patterns. Changing the way we have always done and felt about things is both difficult and challenging. Sometimes the difficult and painful has become familiar and even comfortable, but change is integral and required from the child of God. By committing to read and study His Word on the subject, you will begin to change your understanding. Once insight and discernment come, then obeying His Word to you is the second step and will bring about a change in your behavior. No matter how difficult these changes may be, God has promised to be with us, empowering us toward greater emotional healing and wholeness.

Rooted

Our struggle with boundaries most likely originated in our childhood. At a time when we were not able to analyze what we were going through or even know if there was anything wrong with it, we were made to be responsible for other people's feelings. While growing up we were told to behave or we would make our mothers sad or upset; likewise, if we were naughty or disobedient we had the power to make our father moody or angry. Separateness is not trained, encouraged, or rewarded so we also begin to feel that we are responsible for others and similarly that others are responsible for what is on our property.

Enmeshment is a descriptive word that explains an unhealthy attachment which excludes either party having healthy boundaries or separateness from each other. When this happens within the family, the child accepts responsibility for emotions, moods, and behaviors that are not theirs; what the child is really responsible for becomes completely distorted. If we never learned to set limits, say no, or tell the truth about how we feel we most likely would never have learned to safeguard our souls from the dangers that await us. If a child is never given the permission to disagree with his parents or encouraged to disagree with any facet of family life, an external compliance will be formed. This false compliance makes the child appear to be submissive and obedient, but in reality the child feels angry and resentful. Therefore, many parents are surprised at the open defiance when the child reaches teenage years. Unfortunately, the now rebellious teenager will still not be able to set healthy boundaries. They often find they are unable to set limits on other aspects of their lives, such as substance abuse or abusive romantic relationships and friendships.

Discipline

Henry Cloud and John Townsend say in their book *Boundaries* that "discipline is an external boundary, designed to develop internal boundaries."[2] God disciplines us both with instruction, which should be preventative, and then with correction and consequences when we get it wrong. It is a natural law to reap what we have sowed, and so we learn that our actions will reap consequences. Lots of practice, failing, and learning from our mistakes are the primary ways we learn and mature. "But solid food is for the mature, who by constant use have trained themselves to distinguish good from evil" (Heb. 5:14 NIV).

Christ paid the price for our sins on the cross, so God does not punish us. He does discipline us, however, because He loves us. "Our fathers disciplined us for a little while as they thought best; but God disciplines us for our good, that we may share in His holiness" (Heb. 12:10 NIV). If we have been punished in the past by our natural parents and understood that with punishment comes disapproval (I am a naughty girl/boy), guilt (I made my mother upset), shame (I feel bad about who I am), judgment (I will not be loved anymore), and loss of relationship (I will be abandoned by my parents), then we might become fearful of discipline. But God's discipline never brings isolation or condemnation; we are never in danger of losing His approval and love. His discipline allows us to choose responsibility or suffer the consequences of our actions. Once we understand this, we can safely take responsibility for that which is ours to take—it's our choice! Dr. Edwin Louis Cole said, "Boundaries are to protect life, and not limit pleasures."[3]

FEAR

Boundaries give you freedom because you *choose* to love and you *choose* to give. It is good to sacrifice, to give until it hurts, and to deny yourself for the sake of others; boundaries help make this a choice out of love and not out of fear or resentful compliance. We are meant to be living purposeful lives; but when our boundaries are not intact, we will be driven not by choice but by fear. "In [this] freedom Christ has made us free [and completely liberated us]; stand fast then, and do not be hampered and held ensnared and submit again to a yoke of slavery [which you have once put off]" (Gal. 5:1 AMP).

Fear is most likely the root of why we developed poor or no boundaries in the first place, and fear is what keeps us from changing them. Fear creates our secret boundaries because it doesn't allow us to say *no*; we say *yes* but resent it inside. This prevents us from being honest about our feelings, which is contrary to what the Word tells us: "Therefore, putting away lying, 'Let each one of you speak truth with his neighbor'" (Eph. 4:25).

Cloud and Townsend write that fear causes us to "withdraw passively and quietly instead of communicating an honest no to someone we love. We secretly resent them instead of verbalizing we are angry and how they have hurt us. We will privately endure the pain of someone's irresponsibility instead of telling them how their behavior affects us and other loved ones, information which would be helpful to them."[4] And yet, First

John 4:18 tells us that fear and love cannot coexist. That is why God wants us to have clear and open boundaries; if you are giving based on fear and not on love, you and your relationships will not be blessed. "Each man should give what he has decided in his heart to give, not reluctantly or under compulsion, for God loves a cheerful giver" (2 Cor, 9:7 NIV). God has called us to freedom. Freedom produces good fruit in our lives such as gratitude toward God and love for others. It is always freedom first and service thereafter. We do not serve out of fear but out of freedom. Boundaries guard this freedom, and that is why our pursuit to build better boundaries is of the utmost importance.

SEPARATENESS

Boundaries are about protecting and controlling what is ours and not taking responsibility for that which is not on our property. When someone is able to make you react and cause crisis to your emotions and life, then they are in control of you. This is a clear sign that your boundaries are not in place. When you are not in control of how you react, in words or actions, then this is violating the basic foundation of boundaries which is separateness. God expects us to respond and not react, the difference being that you are in control and you have chosen to respond. If you feel yourself reacting, then it is a sure sign that you need to step back and reevaluate the relationship. This enables you to regain rather than relinquish control of yourself.

Enmeshment may feel like intimacy, but it is not. Intimacy comes from knowing each other very well, accepting shortcomings and differences, and loving and celebrating each other's uniqueness. Enmeshment is attempting to feel and think as if you were the same person. Since quite a bit of one's uniqueness is missed this way, neither person can really be known for whom they are, and this is a very different experience from intimacy.

PASSIVITY

God never rewards passivity. He will always meet us halfway, but He will not do the work for us. If He did, He would be guilty of invading our boundaries. We need to be proactive, recognizing that whatever we ask Him for in prayer, believing, we will receive (see Matt. 21:22). In the parable of the servants with the talents, it was those who had put their talents to work who were rewarded, and the servant who was passive got into trouble.

So take the talent from him, and give it to him who has ten talents. For to everyone who has, more will be given, and he will have abundance; but from him who does not have, even what he has will be taken away. And cast the unprofitable servant into the outer darkness (Matthew 25:28-30).

God is compassionate and comforts those who are fearful, but He will not reward or enable those who are passive and draw back from what He has told them to do. Remember, being fearful is not the problem—stepping back and not *doing* is the problem. God can encourage those who have failed when they try, but He has a problem with those who give up before they have even made an attempt. "Now the just shall live by faith; but if anyone draws back, My soul has no pleasure in him" (Heb. 10:38-39). Boundaries are only established when we choose to be active and assertive.

ENDNOTES

1. *The New Oxford Dictionary of English* (Clarendon Press, 1998), 212 paraphrased.

2. Dr. Henry Cloud and Dr. John Townsend, *Boundaries* (Grand Rapids, MI: Zondervan, 1992), 171.

3. http://www.brainyquote.com/quotes/quotes/e/edwin-louis360075.

4. Dr. Henry Cloud and Dr. John Townsend, *Boundaries* (Grand Rapids, MI: Zondervan, 1992), 101 paraphrased.

Chapter 3

Communication That Counts

———————

*Wise men talk because they have something to say;
fools, because they have to say something.*

–Plato

INTRODUCTION

In The Message version of the Bible, Proverbs 13:17(a) says, "Irresponsible talk makes a real mess of things," and The Living Bible version completes this same proverb, saying, "but reliable communication permits progress." This proverb admonishes us that poor communication causes us confusion and problems, and without reliable skills, we will never progress in our communication with others. Unfortunately for many of us, our childhood, upbringing, and role models have left us with ineffective and inadequate skills, and we are disadvantaged in our relationships. Communication is to our relationship what cement is to our house. It's what keeps the bricks, windows, roof, etc. working together as they should. So if our communication skills are poor, then it is not surprising that our house is falling, or easily torn down. But we are not without hope because God has given us the treasure of His wisdom, understanding, and knowledge that we might grow thereby (see Prov. 24:3). The only things required for change are a hunger for it, humility to accept it, and the person of the Holy Spirit teaching us. I am not proud to admit that I was not always as ready for change as I am now and this hindered my personal growth and relationships.

George Bernard Shaw said, "The single biggest problem in communication is the illusion that it has taken place."[1] One definition of communication is "the successful conveying or sharing of ideas and feelings."[2] We may think we are conveying our ideas and feelings, but are they successfully received? Good communication is learned behavior, and it means extra effort, insights, and skill. Without active change we will always fall back on old, learned patterns and family default positions. I once had an acquaintance who told me quite proudly that he was a good communicator based on the fact that he went to the pub regularly and spoke all night to his mates! Most people believe that they communicate well, but plain "talking" cannot ever be classed as effective communication!

Ineffective communication is often the cause of tremendous gaps in our lives—the messes and miseries we live with, such as loneliness, family problems, job incompetence, dissatisfaction, stress, and illness. Robert Bolton, in *People Skills*, says, "Many people today yearn for warm, affectionate, positive, meaningful relatedness with and to others but seem unable to experience it and this is largely due to poor communication."[3] Unfortunately, the most intense loneliness is often experienced within families where communication has broken down. Couples who go into marriage expecting an enriching, fulfilling, and intimate experience often lack the relational skills to bring about this dream. Those who come from broken families or homes where relationships were strained, dysfunctional, and unhealthy make inner vows that they are going to have something much better than their parents. Sadly, although they have higher expectations, they also have fewer skills.

A relationship that has no flow of communication will be like a river dammed up, stagnating, and eventually toxic. Bolton also states, "Communication is the life blood of any and every relationship. When open, clear, sensitive communication takes place, the relationship is nurtured. When communication is guarded, hostile, or ineffective the relationship falters, deteriorates, and ultimately dies."[4] Communication skills must be learned on purpose no matter what upbringing or background we have had.

COMMUNICATION IS BOTH VERBAL AND NONVERBAL

Writer and famous business thinker Peter F. Drucker said, "The most important thing in communication is to hear what isn't being said."[5] Some research says as little as 7 to 35 percent is communicated with words.[6] Proverbs 20:12 tells us, "The hearing ear and the seeing eye, the Lord has made them both." We communicate consciously and subconsciously with our eyes, facial expressions, and body postures:

- We lift one eyebrow in doubt or disbelief.

- We rub our noses in puzzlement.

- We clasp our arms to isolate ourselves or to protect ourselves.

- We shrug our shoulders for indifference.

- We wink one eye for intimacy.

- We tap our fingers for impatience.

- We slap our foreheads for forgetfulness.

A person cannot "not" communicate; they may have stopped talking, but they haven't stopped communicating. Understanding your own, as well as reading other people's body language, contributes toward good communication. "The look on their countenance witnesses against them" (Isa. 3:9).

VERBAL COMMUNICATION

Communication in any relationship and in any situation can be done in three effective steps: Receive, Reflect, and Respond.

1. Receive

When we become proficient at listening, we have learned to correctly receive the message being sent to us. We would save ourselves from so much trouble if we would just be quiet and listen, look, and learn (see Prov. 21:23). Ecclesiastes 3:7 says, "There is a time to keep silence, and a time to speak." In a typical person's life, up to 70% of our day is spent communicating; of that 70%, writing took up 9%, reading 16%, talking 30%, and listening occupied 45%.[7] It is therefore essential that we listen effectively, yet very few people are great at this skill. Jesus was constantly reminding his followers in the Gospels: "If anyone has ears to hear, let him hear." Then He said to them, "Take heed what you hear" (Mark 4:23-24).

In general communication, we tend to ignore, forget, or misunderstand most of what people tell us. Even worse, people don't really "hear" what is being communicated, verbally or nonverbally, on a deeper level. As the saying goes, too often the words go into one ear and out the other!

Effective listening involves physical posture, eye contact, and a refusal to be distracted by the environment. That is, listen with your whole body. Also, listening involves as little interruption as possible; ask only a few questions and give encouragement to let them know they are being heard correctly. Proverbs 10:19 admonishes us to make listening a priority in our lives over and above that of our talking.

2. Reflect

This is a valuable communication skill. Reflecting is paraphrasing, mirroring back feelings and their meaning, and summarizing what has been said. Before we begin to answer back in a conversation, it is vital that we understand exactly what has been communicated. Too often we display our foolishness by answering a matter before we have fully heard or understood it (see Prov. 18:13). John Powell said, "Listening is a search to find the treasure of the true person as revealed verbally and nonverbally. There is the semantic problem, of course. The words bear a different connotation for you than they do for me. Consequently, I can never tell you what you said, but only what I heard. I will have to rephrase what you have said, and check it out with you to make sure that what left your mind and heart arrived in my mind and heart intact and without distortion."[8]

We often reflect more than we think we do. When someone gives us a telephone number or other details to write down, we automatically repeat what they have said to be sure we heard it correctly. This kind of accuracy-listening-check communicates to our relationships that we have heard, understood, and accepted what they have said. Not only has this skill been essential to me in my significant relationships, but I also use it regularly in my role as pastor and counselor.

Reflection keeps us from falling into the pitfalls of poor communication skills, including recalling past mistakes, not sticking with the challenge at hand and not making one issue bigger than it is. After falling into this trap several times, my husband, Michael, and I have become more proficient at keeping the main thing the main thing! Our disagreements on specific church issues used to invade our home life, and an upgrading of our communication skills was necessary to keep our marriage healthy and happy. In reflection, we make a more concerted effort to understand where the other person is coming from and to not always prove we are right. "Every way of a man is right in his own eyes, but the Lord weighs the hearts" (Prov. 21:2).

3. Respond

This is when we give our opinion, feelings, and thoughts. Unfortunately, this is where most people want to begin. We need to learn to stop thinking about what we're going to say when the other person stops talking, but rather start with receiving then reflecting. As emotions are often very heated in conflict, it is vital to keep the three steps in order and try not to interrupt or get defensive. If they feel we have heard and understood them, they will most likely be more receptive to us. We may be determined to make the other person see our view of things, but if we do this all the time, there will be little focus given to the other person's point of view and nobody will feel heard or understood. Understanding them will also give us the advantage to better explain our side of the argument.

When you respond:

Use "I" messages. Rather than saying things like "You really messed up here," begin statements with "I" and make them about yourself and your feelings. For example, "I feel frustrated when this happens." It's less accusatory so it sparks less defensiveness, and it helps the other person understand your point of view. The less attack, the less counterattack.

Don't hint or be vague. "I really wish I didn't have to cook tonight" or "I'm really tired of cooking" would be so much more effective if you were direct and said, "I really don't feel like cooking tonight because I've had a long, hard week. Do you think you could make something, Honey, or should we get takeout?" Insecure people will hint rather than make a direct statement because it makes them feel less vulnerable and rejected should they get a negative answer. Be straightforward and come right out with it rather than presuming the worst.

Use empathy. When someone comes at you with criticism, it's easy to feel they're wrong and get defensive. While criticism is hard to hear, and is often exaggerated or colored by the other person's emotions, it's important to listen for the other person's pain and respond with empathy for their feelings. Also, look for what is true in what they're saying; that can be valuable information for you.

Own what is yours. Realize that personal responsibility is a strength, and by taking ownership when you are wrong, you will grow in your relationships. If you both share some responsibility in a conflict (which is usually the case), look for and admit to what's yours. It diffuses the situation, sets a good example, and shows maturity. It also often inspires the other person to respond in kind, leading both of you closer to mutual understanding and a solution. "In the mouth of a fool is a rod of pride, but the lips of the wise will preserve them" (Prov. 14:3).

Take a time-out. Sometimes tempers get heated, and it's just too difficult to continue a discussion without it becoming destructive strife. If you feel yourself or your partner starting to get too angry and the argument is no longer constructive, it is best to take a break and give both of you time to cool off. This is also part of good communication. "Even a fool is counted wise when he holds his peace; when he shuts his lips, he is considered perceptive" (Prov. 17:28).

Don't give up. While taking a break from the discussion is sometimes a good idea, always persevere toward a compromise and settlement. If you both approach the situation with a constructive attitude, mutual respect, and a willingness to see the other's point of view or at least to find a solution, you can make progress toward resolution. Unless it's time to give up on the relationship, don't give up on communication.

ENDNOTES

1. http://thinkexist.com/quotation/the_single_biggest_problem_in_communication_is/155222.html.

2. *The New Oxford Dictionary of English* (Gloucestershire, UK: Clarendon Press, 1998), 371.

3. Robert Bolton, *People Skills* (New York, NY: Simon & Schuster, Inc; Touchstone, 1979), 5 paraphrased.

4. Ibid., 6 paraphrased.

5. http://www.brainyquote.com/quotes/authors/p/peter_f_drucker.html.

6. Randall Harrison (1970) *Non-verbal Communication.* Cited in: Robert Bolton, *People Skills* (New York, NY: Simon & Schuster, Inc; Touchstone, 1979), 78.

7. Ralph Nichols & Leonard Stevens, *Are you listening?* (New York, NY: McGraw-Hill, 1957), 6.

8. John Powell, *The Secret of Staying in Love* (Niles, IL: Argus Communications, 1974), 140.

Chapter 4

Dare to Disconnect

—•·••·•—

The hardest word in the English language is goodbye.

—Christ Zois

CLARITY

As humans, we find saying "goodbye" one of the most difficult things we have to do, but we cannot underestimate its importance to our mental health. I have called this chapter Dare to Disconnect because it takes courage and perseverance to make essential changes, including ending a relationship. Making these types of changes in relationships is never easy because it evokes strong emotions such as guilt, hurt and loss. The definition of *disconnect* is "to sever or interrupt or terminate the connection of or between; detach."[1] When a relationship is detrimental or toxic to our emotional, mental, or spiritual well-being, we must be prepared to detach and change the existing rules and boundaries. We may even need to sever or terminate the relationship. We will be discussing both of these aspects in this chapter.

CHALLENGE

It is normal for all relationships to falter and become difficult at times. Jesus gives us this guarantee in Luke 17:1: "It is impossible that no offenses should come." Depending on the relationship, we may be tempted to think that severing or terminating a relationship may be easier than continuing the struggle to maintain it. However, if we had to sever every relationship that became hurtful or difficult or dysfunctional, we may end up with very few or no relationships.

Another challenge we face is to analyze correctly the relationships that really need altering. Those destructive and draining relationships that keep us rooted in the past are usually easy to spot by their negative impact on our lives. But our challenge lies with those relationships that we do not see as being destructive. Long-term relationships often have blind spots attached to them which hinder us from understanding all the dynamics involved. In the story of *Red Riding Hood* by Hans Christian Anderson, clever kids could perhaps ask why little Red Riding Hood did not *know* that the wolf was up to no good when he interrupted her journey. Didn't she know that wolves are bad? But it is one thing to know that wolves are bad and another thing completely to *recognize* them when they come into our worlds. Maybe the wolves are really nice to us, offering some good advice or direction and dressed up as sweet little grandmothers? However, as with this story, we know that wolves are deceptive and flattering and will try to eat us alive.

At some point or another, we all have wolves in our lives, but the challenge comes in evaluating them correctly and in time. Conflict is sure, tests and trials are a given, but understanding their ultimate motive is crucial to our survival and progress. Part of this challenge involves taking an inventory of those who are in our inner circle of friendships because they will always have the greatest influence on our lives. Look to the fruit of the relationship; and if you suspect that something is wrong, take counsel from someone wiser than yourself. All of this will also make us better at discerning others' characters.

CORRECT

T.D. Jakes uses a fabulous illustration in his book *Maximizing the Moment*.[2] If we are holding a cup of tea and not paying much attention to the person who is pouring it or the fact that they have asked us to say "when" or "enough," then we will miss the cue to say "enough!" Before we know it, the tea cup is overflowing and we find ourselves having to clean up a mess. More seriously, we need to ask how many times we react similarly to that in our relationships. When we don't say anything and allow others to determine how much they pour into our lives—how much they use us, how much they distract us from the purpose and destiny of God in our lives, and how much they drain us— they are in control. Our lives are too important to leave it in the hands of anyone else.

When people pour themselves into us, we wish or hope that they will know when it is too much and stop. Wishing, hoping, and even praying will not change this, but taking your God-given control will! Don't wait for a big mess to clean up, with heartache and brokenness, before you jump up and say "enough." We cannot expect others to be responsible for knowing when our cup is full. God in His Word has told us we are the steward of our own souls, and we must take ownership of our heart and guard it with all diligence (see Prov. 4:23).

We endanger our own lives and that of others when we refuse to use the brakes of the car we are driving. To add to this analogy, no one should have the power to move you into the passenger seat of your own life and control your destination. Only you and God should have power over where you are going and how to get there. Likewise, you should always keep your eyes firmly fixed on the road ahead, not peeled sideways at the person sitting next to you. People's opinion and approval must never have this much influence in your life or a head-on collision is just around the corner.

CONFRONT

To confront is simply to see clearly and face directly the essence of a particular relationship.[3] In any potential conflict or war, we must always examine whether the spoils will be worth the conflict. If there are no advantages, the effort of the conflict is not worth it and confrontation is unnecessary. Confronting someone is not something we tend to enjoy, and so we will often avoid it at any cost even to our own detriment. We must be prepared to deal with a matter before it deals with us; and the longer we leave it, the more serious it may become. There are no short-cuts to or escape from just being obedient to what the Holy Spirit has instructed us to do concerning the relationship; this may not be possible without confrontation.

We are fearful of confrontation because we expect anger, hurt, and emotional bruises to follow. Cutting someone out of your life may have short-term pain attached, but with long-term benefits. Visiting the dentist may hurt a little, but it is not "harmful." When you must confront someone, the Holy Spirit will help you to speak the truth in love (see Eph. 4:15). The more secure and mature we become, the more we are able to be assertive and deal with the issues head-on. The world's two patterns are passivity or aggression. The first allows others to walk over us, the second for us to walk over others. But as Christians, we know there is a better way. Healthy, secure relationships can handle the truth spoken in love, and will move forward in strength. Those who do not survive this process were most likely dysfunctional from the start.

COMPROMISE

T.D. Jakes says that compromise is creating win-win situations.[4] Compromise means "a settlement of differences by mutual concessions." Good marriages thrive on mutual concessions because this promotes peace and allows for individuality without total independence. "Be subject to one another out of reverence for Christ (the Messiah, the Anointed one). Wives, be subject (be submissive **and adapt yourselves**) to your own husbands as [a service] to the Lord" (Eph. 5:21-22 AMP). Being subject, adapting, and adjusting to one another is the scriptural basis of every marriage.

It is in marriage that we must persevere and persist toward wholeness, more than in any other relationship. Because marriage is a covenant relationship, it is different from all our other relationships and must be treated differently. Gaining insight and clarity, being challenged and even corrected, confronting where necessary, and promoting compromise are all essential to avoid the divorce that God hates. There are two primary reasons for this:

1. Marriage was meant to be a picture on earth of God's relationship with us, and God will never break His covenant with us.

2. God hates divorce because of the emotional devastation and hurt it causes both partners, the family, and community.

During my university days, I attended a meeting where I was shown a potent illustration of the effect of divorce. The leader took two pieces of paper and glued them together. After waiting for them to dry, he tried to pull them apart again. The glue had done such a good job that the paper would not separate easily. When it finally did, each piece had big holes in it and both had patches where the glue and other paper were still attached. When couples divorce, they are left with gaping holes where once they were covered and whole and other patches where their ex-partner is still imprinted on their souls. Most divorced people will tell you that if compromising, adjusting, and adapting are possible, then everything must be done to avoid the terrible misery that divorce causes everyone involved. As a child of God, be assured that there can never be a divorce between God and you: "For I am persuaded that neither death nor life, nor angels nor principalities nor powers, nor things present nor things to come, nor height nor depth, nor any other created thing, shall be able to separate us from the love of God which is in Christ Jesus our Lord" (Rom. 8:38-39).

CUT OFF

British physician Havelock Ellis said, "All the art of living lies in a fine mingling of letting go and holding on."[5] When relationships are toxic and dysfunctional, when they leave us feeling inadequate and worthless, when they are not going in the same direction as us and hinder us from fulfilling our purpose, when there is only history and no destiny, we need to end them. "For evildoers shall be cut off; but those who wait on the Lord, they shall inherit the earth" (Ps. 37:9). Many times this process is painful and difficult, so we allow ourselves to be manipulated by either our own emotions or those of the other party. We also passively delay the process with dire consequences; all the while hoping things will improve by themselves. There is, however, enormous benefit and release that comes from finally being obedient to the voice of God. On one very memorable occasion, many years ago, when my husband and I cut off a toxic relationship, we found the promises and provision of God flooded our lives. This also served as a complete confirmation that what we had done was correct for us.

When Romans 12:10 instructs us to give preference to one another, it does not mean that God intends for us to lose ourselves in the process. This can be identified by the following rotten fruit:

- Ignoring our own emotions until we can no longer tell what we are feeling.

- Ignoring our preferences so that we eventually forget what is important to us.

- Sacrificing our opinions for the opinions of others.

- Valuing the advice of others over our own convictions and the voice of God.

If you have ticked all of the above, maybe you are in the process of losing your identity, personality, and essential self to please others. Getting someone's approval and acceptance just to make yourself feel valued and loved is never worth this price. If correction is impossible, termination of this relationship is essential.

Finally, do not confuse the loneliness, hurt, guilt, and grief that you experience over a lost relationship with the incorrect assumption that you have made a mistake. These emotions often follow loss of any kind, and they are not an indication that we were wrong to sever the relationship. We can grieve the loss of what we thought we had, or what we thought we could have had, but we do not undo the process based on these emotions. Words alone do not define reality—only behavior does—so we must only recant when we see the fruit of a changed life.

Endnotes

1. http://www.thefreedictionary.com/disconnect.

2. T.D. Jakes, *Maximize the Moment* (New York, NY: G.P. Putnam's Sons, 1999), 11-12 paraphrased.

3. http://www.dictionary.net/confront.

4. T.D. Jakes, *Maximize the Moment* (New York, NY: G.P. Putnam's Sons, 1999), 34 paraphrased.

5. http://www.finestquotes.com/author_quotes-author-Havelock%20Ellis-page-0.htm.

Chapter 5

Evaluating Expectations

———————

INTRODUCTION

Expectations frequently come into play in our relationships, and we experience them most keenly when broken expectations leave us feeling disappointed and hurt. Evaluating and understanding our expectations is essential to building and maintaining healthy relationships. The dictionary defines *expectation* as "the act or state of looking forward or anticipating; a prospect of future good or profit."[1] The Scriptures refer to expectation as a positive, confident anticipation and trust which is twinned with hope. The apostle Paul communicates his expectations of those in the Corinthian church that they may not fail him, whether in good or bad times, and that they would grow and produce good fruit (see 2 Cor. 1:7; 10:15 AMP). In the Amplified version of Philippians 1:20, we see Paul tell us his own expectation that he not let himself down. It is good and right to have expectations of God, ourselves, and others.

Although this definition of expectation refers only to the good and positive, life's difficulties and our experiences may have taught us to expect the bad and to have faith in the negative more than the positive. Expectations can also be based on our childhood or role models. Additionally, some expectations are neither positive nor negative, but they still play a significant role in our lives. For example, if you grew up in a home where your father woke up first every morning and brought you coffee before you got up for school, when you got married you would naturally expect the man in your life to bring you coffee! The temperament of a person may also play a role in how much or how little is expected or even demanded. Personalities who expect a lot from themselves can also demand a lot from others; whereas, the easy-going temperament tends to generally have lower or more realistic expectations of those around them.

These environments we grew up in can be unreliable frames of reference. Furthermore, the media presents us with an unrealistic Hollywood fairytale reference. See these influences for what they really are—false—we must always refer to the Word of God to establish normal and healthy parameters for our relationships and our lives.

UNREALISTIC EXPECTATIONS

Much hurt and disappointment comes from having unrealistic expectations. For example, if our expectations are not based on the promises of God but rather on what we *feel* God should do for us, we will become disappointed with God. Another example is when we set unrealistic goals for ourselves based on a deep need to always please others, which we know to be rooted in our insecurity and fear of rejection. Unfortunately, this results in constant disappointment with self and continued low self-esteem. If we have learned to idealize relationships with others based on role modeling or what Hollywood portrays as being normal, we will also be regularly disappointed with the reality of the relationships around us.

In Luke 24, the disciples are walking on the road to Emmaus and talking with Jesus, although they don't know it is actually Jesus. In verse 21, they tell Jesus of their disappointment in Him: "But we were hoping that it was He who was going to redeem Israel." This disappointment, however, was based on unrealistic expectations that Jesus would deliver them from their political oppression. Their bitter upset and confusion was not at all Jesus' fault because He had never promised He would do this for them. Let's look at some other examples where we might fall into the trap of disappointment based on unrealistic expectations:

- It is realistic to want your spouse to be kind and loving and to express that love, but it is not realistic to want your spouse to be like that all the time.

- It is realistic to expect those with whom we have a close relationship to not maliciously hurt us, but it is unrealistic to think that they are never going to let us down, be insensitive, or hurt us.

- It is realistic to think that our relationships should be fulfilling and meet our emotional needs, but it is unrealistic to think someone should "rescue" us or that they should be completely responsible for our emotional fulfillment and happiness.

- It is realistic to want to have fun and good times with those we love, but it is unrealistic to expect a "happily ever after" with no tough times. It is unrealistic to expect every relationship to stand strong through tests or even survive the challenges they will inevitably face.

- It is realistic to expect other people to put effort into the relationship, and it is unrealistic to think that relationships can survive if they are neglected.

In Matthew, we hear the story of laborers being picked to work in the vineyard, some at the beginning of the day and others at the middle of the day and some at the end of the day. When it comes time to pay them, the Master gives them all the same wages. Those who were employed at the beginning of the day got exactly what they were promised and the owner fulfilled his obligation to them, but they were upset because they expected more. They expected the owner of the vineyard to change his behavior to suit them and their feelings of unfairness. The owner was well within his rights to show generosity to those who came at the end of the day and do with his money as he pleased (see Matt. 20:1-16).

As with these laborers, we get upset and offended when we feel someone has not done things the way we wanted. However, everyone has free will (that even God respects), and we cannot dictate or control others to suit our needs or wants. Learning how to correctly assess situations and maintain realistic expectations will help us avoid disappointment and protect relationships. Lowering expectations can also prevent resentment and hurt, and it may protect the remaining positive aspects of the relationship.

I remember speaking with a friend who was distraught over the death of her father and how her mother has changed so much as a result of their bereavement. Even after a considerable amount of time, there was constant strife, hurt, and disappointment between my friend and her mother. I counseled her to stop basing her expectations on their past history as mother and daughter and to lower her expectations of the relationship. The relationship immediately improved when my friend started valuing what was left of the relationship, rather than being constantly disappointed as to what was no longer there.

UNSPOKEN EXPECTATIONS

One of the greatest challenges relationships face is that everyone has different ideas about how much they want to put into their relationships and how much they want out of them. Different types of relationships need different levels of effort, so make sure you know what others expect from you. Do you know what you expect and how to verbalize your expectations? Unspoken expectations cause constant disappointment and ultimately lead to the breakdown of the relationship. We expect others to know what we want. We don't want to risk rejection by being vulnerable and communicating our thoughts. We allow ourselves to think we are keeping the peace and thereby protecting the relationship, but many times we are harming it. Have the courage to put away all falsity, as the apostle Paul instructs, and speak the truth with your neighbor (see Eph. 4:25).

The older brother in the parable of the lost son became disappointed, angry, and even bitter with his father and his younger brother. We do not know exactly his motive for remaining silent and not communicating his needs and expectations to his father, but we can surmise that he did not want to add to his father's heartache. As we read in the parable, the father tells his son that his expectations were realistic and the father would have been happy to fulfill them had he known of them. However, the son's expectation that his father would not be overjoyed and generous with his prodigal son is unrealistic and based only on his own disappointment and resentment. (See Luke 15:11-32.) What uncommunicated expectations in your relationships have led to disappointment? Which have given way to resentment or bitterness?

Don't assume that those around you know what you expect from your relationships. Tell them clearly and specifically what your most important expectations are. Do not, however, give them an impossible list that will only leave them feeling defensive and inadequate; be wise not to damage the relationship. Find out and listen to what they expect as well. They too might not have thought to verbalize their expectations. Use the communication skills from Chapter 3 (Receive, Reflect, Respond) and success will come with consistent and continued effort. Communicating our expectations is as vital to our relationships as oxygen is to our physical bodies.

UNFULFILLED EXPECTATIONS

If our expectations were unfulfilled—whether they were realistic or unrealistic, spoken or unspoken—we are still left dealing with loss, grief, disappointment, and bitterness. This is common to all mankind. If we look at King David's family story in Second Samuel 13-14, we see that he had every right to be heartbroken. Both his first and third-born sons betrayed him bitterly. His third son, Absalom, was his father's pride and joy and was praised for his good looks (see 2 Sam. 14:25). But Absalom led a rebellion against his father, forcing David to flee for his life. David must have had intense feelings of inadequacy and humiliation, both as a father and as a king. His failure was not only private but the cause of great public humiliation: "So the king arose and tore his garments and lay on the ground" (2 Sam. 13:31).

Amidst this crisis, David wrote:

> *My soul, wait silently for God alone, for **my expectation is from Him**. He only is my rock and my salvation; He is my defense; I shall not be moved. In God is my salvation and my glory; the rock of my strength, and my refuge, is in God. Trust in Him at all times, you people; Pour out your heart before Him; God is a refuge for us. Surely men of low degree are a vapor, Men of high degree are a lie; if they are weighed on the scales, they are altogether lighter than vapor. Do not trust in oppression, nor vainly hope in robbery; if riches increase, do not set your heart on them. God has spoken once, twice I have heard this: That power belongs to God. Also to You, O Lord, belongs mercy; for You render to each one according to his work* (Psalm 62:5-12).

This psalm gives us great insight into how he manages to process his shattered dreams:

- David understood the cleansing value of pouring his heart out before God his Savior. He did not run *from* God, but instead he ran to Him. He held nothing back in his confession and expressed all his feelings. When we find such a trusted confidant to do this with and pray for one another, we will be healed (see James 5:16). This is where the Spirit of God begins to work.

- This psalm shows us how David trusts God in the good times and in the bad. Whether he was sitting on his throne in Jerusalem or running for his life, he trusted and praised God at all times. One of my favorite sayings in church is,

"There are only two times when we praise God: when we feel like it and when we don't!"

- Third, we clearly see that David has learned not to trust in men. "God alone" was His rock, defense, and constant. Betrayal is an effective reminder that people will always fail us in one way or another. We must not expect friends, family, spouses, or jobs to do for us what only God can do—never let us down!

- David didn't allow hard times to make him bitter or hard-hearted. Likewise, we cannot allow the enemy to use our bitterness to rob us of hope. We need to be aware that shattered expectations are one of satan's favorite schemes against us. Many have turned away from God because they're angry and disappointed.

GREAT EXPECTATIONS

In high school, I loved studying the novel *Great Expectations* by Charles Dickens. In this story, one of the main characters, Pip, a poor boy with no prospects of a better life, gets an undeserved and unexpected inheritance. Immediately his life changes, and we read about him as a young man with a great future. We, too, by the grace of God have received an undeserved inheritance through Jesus. Jeremiah 29:11 speaks about our future prospects: "'For I know the thoughts that I think toward you,' says the Lord, 'thoughts of peace and not of evil, to give you a future and a hope.'"

All our greatest expectations must be based on the Word of God and what He can do for us. He can then turn our disappointment around so we can become refocused and reappointed. "[For it is He] Who rescued and saved us from such a perilous death, and He will still rescue and save us; in and on Him we have set our hope (our joyful and confident expectation) that He will again deliver us [from danger and destruction and draw us to Himself]" (2 Cor. 1:10 AMP).

ENDNOTE

1. http://dictionary.reference.com/browse/expectation.

Chapter 6

Fabulous Friendships

———◆◆◆———

My best friend is the one who brings out the best in me.

—Henry Ford

INTRODUCTION

It is commonly known that two of the greatest influences in our lives are what we read and who we choose to spend our time with—our friends. Therefore, it is certainly worthwhile to find out what the Word of God says concerning this specific type of relationship and its importance to us. The dictionary defines *friendship* as "a friendly relation or intimacy" and *friend* as "an acquaintance or someone highly esteemed." The New Testament uses several words for *friend*, including "friend, companion, comrade, and neighbor." We also see kinship terms, such as brother, mother, or child, which refer to people outside the family for whom there is a special affection. For example, the apostle Paul referred to Timothy as his beloved son (see 1 Cor. 4:17).

FRIENDSHIP WITH GOD

I love the song we sing in church called "I Am a Friend of God" by Israel Houghton. It reminds me how privileged I am to be His special friend! Friendship with God is not something unattainable or irreverent to expect, but it is something that we have if we do as He has commanded us (see John 15:14). Abraham also gained the title *"friend of God"* by his faith and obedience (see James 2:23). By contrast, when we are a friend of the world we are immediately disqualified from the possibility of friendship with God (see James 4:4).

FRIENDSHIP WITH PEOPLE

God understands that a relationship with Him alone is insufficient to meet our need for companionship (see Gen. 2:18). The Scriptures give accounts of the benefits of a friendship in all different kinds of circumstances.

> *Two are better than one, because they have a good reward for their labor. For if they fall, one will lift up his companion. But woe to him who is alone when he falls, for he has no one to help him up. Again, if two lie down together, they will keep warm; but how can one be warm alone? Though one may be overpowered by another, two can withstand him. And a threefold cord is not quickly broken* (Ecclesiastes 4:9-12).

We all have a longing for deep, meaningful, and loyal friendships. It does not take much to convince us that "two is better than one." Our God-given temperaments, however, will influence our view on friendships and how we respond to them. Let us look at the four main temperaments and their friendship characteristics:

- *The Sanguine:* Makes friends easily; loves people; thrives on compliments; seems exciting; envied by others; doesn't hold grudges; apologizes quickly; prevents dull moments; likes spontaneous activities.

- *The Melancholic:* Makes friends cautiously; content to stay in the background; avoids causing attention; faithful and devoted; will listen to complaints; can solve other's problems; deep concern for other people; moved to tears with compassion; seeks ideal mate.

- *The Choleric:* Has little need for friends; will work for group activity; will lead and organize; is usually right; excels in emergencies.

- *The Phlegmatic:* Easy to get along with; pleasant and enjoyable; inoffensive; good listener; dry sense of humor; enjoys watching people; has many friends; has compassion and concern.[1]

I recently read and agreed with an article that said, "We usually choose a partner who is opposite in temperament to us as this brings completion but we choose our friends based on similarity."[2] Our friends tend to have similar likes, strengths, and weaknesses that affirm and validate us. Every type of temperament is important, and none is better or worse than the others. It is noteworthy that although our spouse should be our best friend, he or she should not be our *only* friend. Having close friendships does not subtract from our marriage, but should strengthen and enrich it. When a couple only relates to each other, they end up placing unrealistic demands on one other causing strife and damage to their relationship.

DIFFERENT LEVELS OF FRIENDSHIPS

From the Bible, we are able to ascertain that there are different levels of friendships involving different types of components. On my husband's iPhone, he has me earmarked as "AAA," which is truly the highest of honors. I am blessed to be his triple A! Likewise, we can categorize our friendships into three A's:

- The A level of friendship is Association. This is an acquaintance or neighbor with whom we have a connection, but there is no specific loyalty (see Rom. 15:2).

- The AA friendship is Allegiance. At a deeper level, the idea of friendship contains association, as well as allegiance and loyalty (see 1 Kings 5:1; John 19:12). The friend who sticks closer than a brother displays this loyalty in Proverbs 18:24 and is found in an AA friendship.

- Our third and deepest level, an AAA friendship, is Affection. It means there is a fond attachment, devotion, and love. It contains all the components of association and allegiance and affection (see 1 Sam. 18:1; Phil. 4:1).

JESUS' EXAMPLE

Jesus enjoyed all three levels of friendships while here on earth, and the Bible gives us examples of His deepest relationships. The apostle John was "the disciple whom He loved" (John 19:26). Also, in John 11:3, we see His close friendship with Lazarus. And in John 15:13-15, Jesus not only addresses His disciples as friends, but He also displays all the elements of a close and affectionate relationship: "Greater love has no one than this, than to lay down one's life for his friends. You are My friends if you do whatever I command you." He opens up his heart and shares with them the deeper meaning of His life, ministry, and ultimate sacrifice on the cross. Even today, when you and I do what He commands, we are His friend of the AAA kind.

THE VALUE

Now that we have seen the meaningful friendships Jesus had, we can look forward to new and deeper friendships, and we can appreciate even more the ones we already have. Here are 5 C's to help us become more purpose-driven and spirit-led in this area of our relationships:

- *Close Companionship*: "God said, 'It's not good for the Man to be alone; I'll make him a helper, a companion'" (Gen. 2:18 TM). Fun time with friends is important because it helps keep us balanced between work and play. It refreshes and relaxes us so that we do not burn out from stress or too much hard work.

- *Comforting Counsel:* "Ointment and perfume delight the heart, and the sweetness of a man's friend gives delight by hearty counsel" (Prov. 27:9). Friends know us well enough that we don't have to explain ourselves, and we can count on them for comfort and encouragement.

- *Challenge and Change:* "As iron sharpens iron, so a man sharpens the countenance of his friend" (Prov. 27:17). Our friends push us to become all we can become in God so we do not settle for less. Accountability with them will also help protect us.

- *Crisis or Calamity:* "Do not forsake your own friend or your father's friend, Nor go to your brother's house in the day of your calamity; Better is a neighbor nearby than a brother far away" (Prov. 27:10). In times of trouble, when it truly counts, friends depend on each other. Deposits made into the friendship during the good times ensures withdrawals can be made in the difficult times. "A friend loves at all times, and a brother is born for adversity" (Prov. 17:17).

- *Constructive Criticism:* "Faithful are the wounds of a friend; but the kisses of an enemy are deceitful" (Prov. 27:6). Friends will risk telling us the truth because they want what is best for us. As they speak the truth to us in love, we need to be wise enough to listen.

THE DANGERS

Understanding the unlimited blessing and value of our Holy Spirit-inspired and anointed friendships, we realize that the enemy will invest a great deal in destroying them. All of us have experienced the pain of a broken or dysfunctional friendship. It is usually not our associates or acquaintances that have this power over us, but rather those with whom we have deep affection and a meaningful connection. Let us look at some of the effects of friendships that go wrong:

- Our character is broken down through negative influences (see Prov. 1:10-19; 4:14-19; 22:24).

- Friends prove false, using flattery and pretending affection and loyalty from ulterior motives (see Prov. 19:4; Ps. 5:9).

- Friendships break down through gossip, causing strife, hurt, and rejection (see Prov. 16:28; 17:9).

- Friends may abandon us in our time of need and trouble (see Ps. 38:11).

- Friends can make our suffering and grief worse through misunderstanding (see Job 19:21-22).

We must also stay alert and discerning of the devil's scheme to destroy us through the intimacy that comes from our closest friends. Many of us do not discern that the loneliness we are experiencing, whether we are married or not, makes us vulnerable to overstepping the intimacy boundary with close friendships. A positive, healthy, and deep friendship can quickly turn into an adulterous one when the emotional intimacy and connectedness leads to physical and sexual intimacy. As sin quickly produces death, there are many whose lives and destinies have been destroyed by this scheme of the enemy.

THE SKILLS

It seems that the necessary skills for such an important aspect of our lives—creating and maintaining positive, influential friendships—would have been taught to us early on. However, I have discovered that this has not occurred for many of us. A large percentage of God's people are inadequate in their friendship skills. I pray these simple instructions from God's Word will enhance your skills, no matter at what level you find yourself, and protect you from the potential dangers:

- Let Luke 6:31 become your golden rule for all relationships: "And just as you want men to do to you, you also do to them likewise." Treat your friends as you would have them treat you; not only will you become the best friend they have, but they will become the best friend you ever had.

- Your attitude and disposition are of the utmost importance as you will only reap what you sow (see Gal. 6:7). Proverbs 18:24 also gives us a basic instruction: "A man that hath friends must show himself friendly." Smile and be happy so that people will want to be around you. You cannot be self-pitying, depressed, or self-involved and expect to have great friends; this will be too much like hard work for anyone.

- Neither passivity nor aggression will build positive friendships. Be assertive and direct without being rude or judgmental. Many times, we would sacrifice good friendships because we are too scared to share how we feel. If you find you are doing this, your boundaries need upgrading. Do not live with resentful compliance and blame friends when it's not their fault or problem. "So the Lord spoke to Moses face to face, as a man speaks to his friend" (Exod. 33:11).

- Deep and meaningful friendships can only be built with the solid foundation of genuineness. Ephesians 4:25 says, "We are to put away our falsehood and be truthful with those we love." Being real and genuine comes with time, trust, and self-insight. No one likes someone who they know is being false.

- God the Father gave us the greatest gift He could in His son Jesus, and Jesus in turn gave us His greatest gift of dying on the cross (see John 15:13). Do not focus on what you want to get or receive out of the friendship. Focus rather what you can give. Great friendships are built on giving and sacrificing our time, our resources, and most importantly ourselves. Allowing yourself to be vulnerable and transparent with trusted friends, so they in turn will share their hearts with you, is all part of what Jesus did in His friendships: "No longer do I call you servants, for a servant does not know what his master is doing; but I have called you friends, for all things that I heard from My Father I have made known to you" (John 15:15).

You can make more friends in two months by becoming interested in other people than you can in two years by trying to get other people interested in you. —Dale Carnegie

ENDNOTES

1. http://en.wikipedia.org/wiki/Four_Temperaments.

2. www.foryourmarriage.org/interior_template.asp?id=20399041.

Chapter 7

Given to Games

—•—••—•—

As children, one of the first things we learn is how to play games. Most children will spend endless hours playing games by themselves, with friends, and in groups. Games are used for fun and relaxation, as well as for educational purposes. One of the things I love most about Christmas in England is playing games with our family and friends. This produces such *gezelligheid* (as the Dutch would say) or "coziness." However, when adults play negative emotional games with each other, the outcome is not so positive.

The first and most powerful role we are introduced to, and one of the most influential of our lives, is the Child Role. It can be one role that many people never outgrow. The Bible talks a lot about children and the process of maturing and growing up. The apostle Paul, in First Corinthians 13:11, admonishes us to put away childish things: "When I was a child, I spoke as a child, I understood as a child, I thought as a child; but when I became a man, **I put away childish things.**" In Luke 18:17, however, we are instructed to have child-like faith in order to enter the Kingdom of God. Therefore, we need to distinguish between what the Bible calls "childish" and "child-like."

Children from good environments are carefree, fun-loving, and easily trusting. To their teachers, they are obedient and teachable (see 1 Peter 1:14), and they have no malice or guile as they are ignorant of evil (see 1 Cor. 14:20). In all these ways, we are to copy their example and be child-like and uncomplicated in our faith toward God. Our Christian character is to have no guile or malice. In our Christian walk, we are to be carefree of worries and ignorant of evil. However, children also have no wisdom and are foolish (see Prov. 22:15). In this way, we are never meant to stay child-like. Instead, as the apostle Paul reproaches us, we are to be mature in our understanding (see 1 Cor. 14:20). Children are also easily led astray, as Ephesians 4:14 warns: "**We should no longer be children,** tossed to and fro and carried about with every wind of doctrine, by the trickery of men, in the cunning craftiness of deceitful plotting." The Bible explains that childishness is not fitting for a mature man or woman of God, and it is only in trust and innocence that we forever retain our child-like attitude.

SORE SPOTS

As babes, we come into our world helpless, depending on and needing both physical and emotional relationships. As we are made in the very image and likeness of a relational God and were made for relationship, the thought and experience of being cut off from the support and affection of those we love and depend on can be almost unbearable. During our many childhood experiences, all of us will, at some time, experience disapproval, rejection, loss, guilt, abandonment, and pain. Even seemingly normal family experiences can leave us with emotional baggage that we end up carrying with us for the rest of our lives. This in turn creates in us a fear of these things.

If you have often wondered what made you, as opposed to anyone else, susceptible to negative influences and games in your life, then you need to understand the principle of what I like to call "sore spots." Each one of us develops sore spots, which are areas that are charged with our unfinished emotional business, stored up resentments, guilt, pain, insecurities, and vulnerabilities. Our temperament plus our experiences combine to create our unique sore spots. These feelings and memories have been collected over our lifetime and can become activated by triggers in our current lives. Another term that I have heard used for sore spots is "landmine." This word helps us to understand that when we accidentally or subconsciously "stand" on one, our rational thoughts are overruled by the raw emotion of unresolved issues in our past. These landmines are places where emotions are stuffed and forgotten; time cannot heal in landmines, and the suppressed emotions often gain in power. We may not always remember what exactly led to our unique landmines being developed, as it may be the amalgamation of complicated experiences, but we certainly feel it when it is activated.

In the well-known research done with conditioned reflexes, referred to as Pavlov's dogs, dogs were taught to salivate merely at the sound of a bell in expectation of food rather than at food itself.[1] In much the same way, we exhibit conditioned reflexes whenever we go through a situation that reminds us of the original fear we experienced. The unresolved original fear from yesteryear makes us succumb to pressure from those around us in our present lives. Our past is not irrelevant—it plays a very important role—and it can interfere with our ability to handle the stress and upset of our present-day lives. We may understand as adults that these things took place decades ago, but to the child inside of us all, it's as though they happened yesterday. Such emotional memories can keep us locked into *reacting* out of history and habit, rather than *responding* out of growth and destiny.

So the scene was set years ago, and life experiences have left us vulnerable to the games people play. In order to protect ourselves and others from standing on our landmines, which we will do at any cost, we ironically open ourselves up to dysfunctional social games. If any of the statements below describe you, you are most likely vulnerable to such games:

- An excessive need for approval.

- An intense fear of anger.

- A need for peace at any cost.

- A tendency to take too much responsibility for other people's lives.

- A high level of self-doubt and frequent apologizing.

None of these are harmful in balance and moderation. It is not wrong to want to please those you love or pursue peace in your relationships; neither is it wrong to have a good dose of humility. However, when these qualities become extreme, as we fear abandonment through the loss of approval or love, then they will battle against our intelligent, confident, and assertive selves. The very thing we have put in place to protect us is the thing that damages us!

GAMES

Sometimes we are very aware of the games we are involved in, but other times we are confused and ignorant of the mystery surrounding these interpersonal dynamics. There are many types of games, but for simplicity we will place them in three different categories:

Fun games are important as they produce a carefree attitude. They are a means to have fun and laugh in our relationships, while recharging our depleted emotional batteries at the same time. As the child within us is celebrated and enjoyed, fun games are essential to our well-being. Our youth pastor, Scott, has surprised his lovely wife with many a romantic and fun game on Valentine's Day. One year, I remember him hiding small love gifts for Faye all over Exeter, with little clues for her to find throughout the day.

Harmless games are those that we all play from time to time, either on the giving or receiving end, and happen in the healthiest of relationships. We develop these games to get people to do what we want them to do, but there are no dire consequences when people do not comply. For example, we might say, "I wish someone would open the window" instead of "Could you please open the window?" Almost all of us find it hard to be direct sometimes because this requires becoming vulnerable and risking rejection, or feelings of anger. Hinting at what we want is also less risky than coming across needy or aggressive; we can more easily explain away the discomfort caused by a negative response. We hope others will read between the lines and figure out what we want. "I'd really like to come home to a tidy house" or "I feel like a cup of tea" or "The dog needs to go out" are common examples of hinting statements. We even hint with nonverbal clues, such as sighs, and pouts.

Power games are games played with demands, pressure, and negative responses that are destructive to any relationship. Our own private sore spots sabotage us when they are triggered by feelings of fear, obligation, and guilt, and compel us to give into demands and pressure. Simply put, these power games are played by those aiming to control and manipulate others. Unfortunately, we may not have realized that by always giving in, by not confronting or ignoring such behavior, we have taught and even trained them that their behavior is acceptable to us. Every time we accept discomfort and reward bad behavior, we are yielding a bit of our dignity and self-respect. Remember, manipulation always takes two people.

Recognizable power games may include the following:

- Those using strong emotional blackmail to have their way with us, saying things like: "If you really loved me..." or

"Don't leave me or I'll..." or "You're the only one who can help me..." or "I could make things easy for you if you'd just..."

- Those using fear to let us know that if we don't play the game with them they are going to punish us. They let us know exactly what they want and our dire consequences should we not comply. They express themselves aggressively or smoulder in silence; but, either way, the anger they feel is directed at us. Our intense fear of their anger makes us compliant every time.

- Those who turn their threats inwardly and let us know what they will do to themselves if we don't play. Their games produce fear for their well-being and our guilt overtakes any rational thinking as we succumb to the pressure.

- Those who play the blame-game and readily make us feel guilty for not taking responsibility for their lives. Our need for approval and poor sense of boundaries once again ensures our compliance to do what they require.

- Those who put us through tests and promise something wonderful if we'll just give them what they want and play their way all the time!

Most games depend largely on our feelings of guilt, fear, and obligation. Many of us have lost our ability to discern between invalid accusation and reality, and we have come to own the copyright to guilt in all our relationships. Our God-given "guilt-reactor" is dysfunctional, and in order for any of us to discontinue playing any of the above power games with those in our lives, we must first work on repairing it!

GROWING UP IN ALL THINGS

God does not want us to be ignorant in these matters. He wants our understanding to become mature and for us to realize how we become drained, resentful, angry, and defeated in our everyday lives. Ephesians 4:14-15 says, "We should no longer be children, tossed to and fro and carried about with every wind of doctrine, by the trickery of men, in the cunning craftiness of deceitful plotting, but, speaking the truth in love, **may grow up in all things into Him who is the head—Christ.**"

As we grow up into Jesus, we also grow in wisdom and boldness to persevere into the freedom He has won for us. Galatians 5:1 encourages us, "Stand fast therefore in the liberty by which Christ has made us free, and do not be entangled again with a yoke of bondage." The adrenalin that fear produces when we consider making changes will cause us to have a "flight or fight" response.[2] Stop taking the flight option that makes you want to run and hide. This will only reinforce old patterns of pretending that the problem is not as bad as it seems or that it will be solved somehow by itself. Rather choose to fight and stand fast against the bondage you know to be ruling and ruining your life. "Peace at any price" is too high a price to pay for your self-respect. Ensure that the changes you implement are not too radical that you may not be able to sustain them, and be obedient to the Spirit of God who instructs you to just take the next step.

Let us have the commitment and courage to take responsibility for the part we have played in the childish and destructive power games and to press toward the goal of freedom, growth, and maturing in God. Change may be painful, but as children's growing pains are temporary and healthy, so too will ours be. I pray that Philippians 3:12-15 encourages you.

> *Brethren, I do not count myself to have apprehended; but one thing I do, forgetting those things which are behind and reaching forward to those things which are ahead, I press toward the goal for the prize of the upward call of God in Christ Jesus.*

ENDNOTES

1. www.ui.edu/acad/psych/Millis/History/2003/Classical-Conditioning.htm.

2. http://www.thebodysoulconnection.com/EducationCenter/fight.html.

Chapter 8

Heavenly Humor

You can turn painful situations around through laughter.
If you can find humor in anything,
even poverty, you can survive it.

–Bill Cosby

INTRODUCTION

God created us with a capacity for humor, joy, and laughter, and He then gave us the relationships and blessings of life with which to enjoy ourselves. Ultimately, everything good comes from our heavenly Father, and in His very presence there is no small or half-measure of joy, as Psalm 16:11 tells us, "In Your presence is **fullness of joy.**" Although there is no reference in the Bible to humor, I believe that His heavenly humor consists of all the scriptural words like gladness, merry heart, rejoice, and laughter. In fact, one of my favorite Greek definitions for *joy* is "calm delight."[1] So when we talk about God's heavenly humor, we are not necessarily talking about the infrequent "flying from the chandeliers" experiences of joy, but rather the consistent and balanced experience of joy that permeates gently, but significantly, into every one of our relationships.

Jesus is our example and standard to imitate (see Eph. 5:1). He not only was able to have fun at a wedding feast, but He also did not lose His joy throughout His three years of difficult ministry and we read of Him being exceedingly joyful and exuberant in the Holy Spirit (see John 2:2 and Luke 10:21). We get our early church example from the disciples in Acts 13:52, where we see the disciples having no problem with being happy and joyous: "And the disciples were filled with joy and with the Holy Spirit."

JOY IN OUR HEAVENLY RELATIONSHIP

Swiss theologian Karl Barth said, "Laughter is the closest thing to the grace of God."[2] The joy of the Lord is an integral and vital part of our relationship with God. In fact, Romans 14:17 makes it clear that God's Kingdom is not about the natural or carnal things: "For the kingdom of God is not eating and drinking, but righteousness and peace and joy in the Holy Spirit." Joy is not circumstantial like happiness, but rather it is a supernatural empowering in the Holy Spirit to live the victorious Christian life. We first experience and receive the joy of the Lord at salvation (see Isa. 12:3) but if we are not continually filling ourselves with His Holy Spirit then we, like the psalmist, will have to cry to God to restore it to us. "Restore to me the joy of Your salvation, and uphold me by Your generous Spirit" (Ps. 51:12).

During times when we allow our thought life to be undisciplined and we become burdened by our cares and concerns, we won't feel like being joyful. But rejoicing is not a matter of feelings; it is a matter of choice and obedience to God's Word. The decision must be made first, and then, like the donkey obeying its master, the feelings will follow. The apostle Paul does not make it an option, and in Philippians 4:4 he instructs us, "Rejoice in the Lord always. Again I will say, rejoice!" Rejoicing is as much a part of our faith walk as prayer is. Psalm 27:6 speaks about this sacrifice of rejoicing, as we in faith believe God will bring the victory that He has promised: "And now my head shall be lifted up above my enemies all around me; Therefore I will offer sacrifices of joy in His tabernacle; I will sing, yes, I will sing praises to the Lord." We may not have control over our circumstances, but making the right decision to rejoice, even when we don't feel like it, will bring great blessings and fruit in our lives.

Too often we forget everything He has done for us. If there is joy missing in your life, then perhaps thanksgiving is also missing. Psalm 126:2-3 says, "Then our mouth was filled with laughter, and our tongue with singing. Then they said among the nations, 'The Lord has done great things for them.' The Lord has done great things for us, and we are glad."

During my time at university in 1984, I was attending a Christian meeting. After we had finished watching a teaching video, I had an experience in the "exuberant joy in the Holy Spirit," just like Jesus in Luke 10:21—and I will never forget it. Although I had never seen one Scripture or one incident of this happening in church, I started laughing out loud at a thought I had as if it was the funniest thing I had ever heard. It was as if I overheard the enemy say that he was going to destroy my life and destiny. The more I thought about it, the more hysterically funny, ridiculous, and ludicrous it became to me. How could the devil ever think that he would destroy my life while God was holding me in the palm of His hand? (See John 10:29.) How could he begin to imagine that he would succeed while God Himself had bought me with the precious blood of His Son and I was His? (See First Corinthians 6:19-20.) I do not remember how long I laughed or what those around me thought of my behavior (especially as making myself the center of attention is out of character for me), but I knew it was an experience completely from Heaven itself. It was only much later that I discovered God does exactly this Himself in Heaven. "He who sits in the heavens laughs; the Lord has them in derision [and in supreme contempt He mocks them]" (Ps. 2:4 AMP).

This experience, which the disciples also had (see Acts 13:52), has brought me much good fruit. To this day, I remind myself that when tests and trials come to destroy me, I know I am safe in His hands and that He will always take care of me. This joy is still available to me, and on many occasions I tap into it; it is not based in my circumstances, but rather on Him who lives inside of me (see John 7:38). It is the enemy's intent to destroy me, but I am completely convinced that my future is secure in God's Hand. You, too, can laugh at your fears over those who would try to destroy your life and destiny in God. You, too, can have this experience and be filled with the joy and His Holy Spirit as He is the free gift of God to us who believe (see Luke 11:15). You, too, have a secure future in Him, and we can all laugh at the days to come. As the psalmist said in Psalm 5:11, "But let all those rejoice who put their trust in You; Let them ever shout for joy, because You defend them; Let those also who love Your name be joyful in You."

JOY IN OUR RELATIONSHIP WITH OURSELVES

Napoleon Bonaparte said, "We must laugh at man, to avoid crying for him."[3] Many of God's people take themselves far too seriously. Admonishing ourselves from time to time to lighten up and laugh at our silly mistakes would be extremely beneficial to our emotional health. Without joy we have no strength, and without strength we are unable to endure the tests and trials that come our way. Nehemiah 8:10 instructs us, "Do not sorrow, for the joy of the Lord is your strength." Proverbs 31:10 boasts of the Woman of Great Price with whom none could compare, and verse 25 says of her: "Strength and honor are her clothing; she shall rejoice in time to come."

The stresses of everyday life can be very draining and tiring. Many of us struggle at times just to make it through our days, being pulled on from every direction. We certainly do need to know the power of God's strength in our lives, not only to survive, but to be overcomers in this life (see 1 John 5:3-5). We have already read that in "His presence is fullness of joy" and that "this joy will provide me with the strength I need." God's plan is to give me the strength I need by providing me the joy of His presence. The Amplified version of Acts 3:19 witnesses the truth that when I practice the presence of God in my life, I will be refreshed from the heat of my tests and trials of everyday life: "So repent (change your mind and purpose); turn around and return [to God], that your sins may be erased (blotted out, wiped clean), that times of refreshing (of recovering from the effects of heat, of reviving with fresh air) may come from the presence of the Lord."

Matthew Henry's commentary on Proverbs 17:22, "A merry heart does good, like medicine," says this: "It is healthful to be cheerful. The Lord is for the body, and has provided for it, not only meat, but medicine, and has here told us that the best medicine is a merry heart, not a heart addicted to vain, carnal, sensual mirth. But rather he (Solomon) means a heart rejoicing in God, and serving him with gladness, and then taking the comfort of outward enjoyments and particularly that of pleasant conversation. It is a great mercy that God gives us leave to be cheerful and cause to be cheerful, especially if by his grace he gives us hearts to be cheerful."[4] This commentary confirms that we were created by God with the capacity and need for fun. It also states clearly that such fun must not include unclean entertainment or amusement, but only that which produces the good fruits of refreshment, strength, and health for our bodies.

JOY IN OUR RELATIONSHIPS WITH OTHERS

The world's standard of pleasure cannot be celebrated by God's people for it is often debauchery to us. If we need to abuse substances such as alcohol to be the fun-loving people we want to be, then First Peter 4:3 will rebuke us: "You've already put in your time in that God-ignorant way of life, partying night after night, a drunken and profligate life. Now it's time to be done with it for good" (TM). By another witness, we see that such things are not God's ways: "And do not be drunk with wine, in which is dissipation; but be filled with the Spirit" (Eph. 5:18-20). The devil cannot produce true joy as he can only distort that which God creates.

Winston Churchill quipped, "A joke is a very serious thing."[5] When we are so boring, serious, lazy, and unimaginative in our play time with others, we act like God does not want His people to enjoy themselves. Jesus tells us in John 10:10, "I came that they may have and enjoy life, and have it in abundance (to the full, till it overflows)" (AMP). As God's people, we are poor witnesses if we do not fully appreciate our fun times with others. Our friends and those we do life with should want to be around us because we make the effort to be cheerful and creative in our pleasure activities, and we generally just have a continual good time! (See Proverbs 15:15). How is our demeanor and attitude? What is the first thing people notice when we greet them? We cannot expect people to want to be friends with us if we are always looking sad and afflicted, moaning about everything in our lives. In order to have friends, the Bible tells us to be friendly—and with friendliness comes a smile which is a cheerful countenance and disposition (see Prov. 15:13; 18:24).

Being too serious and working all the time will only lead to dysfunctional relationships. Hard work is to be applauded, but is this balanced with quality play time? An inability to relax, laugh, and take pleasure from others is an indication that we might not know how to embrace the fun-loving, playful child within each of us. Even if you did not have a carefree fun-loving childhood, it is never too late to redeem that time in this area of your life. Ask the Holy Spirit to help you enjoy life in all its abundance and to teach you how to have fun, and then you will find that Job 8:21 will come true for you: "He will yet fill your mouth with laughing, and your lips with rejoicing."

He who laughs, lasts. –Anonymous

ENDNOTES

1. http://bibletools.org/index.cfm/fuseaction/Lexicon. show/ID/G5479/chara.htm.

61

2. http://quotationsbook.com/quote/22457/.

3. http://quotationsbook.com/quote/19820/.

4. Matthew Henry, *Matthew Henry's Commentary on the Whole Bible* (Peabody, MA: Hendrickson Publishers, Inc., 1991), 764.

5. http://thinkexist.com/quotation/a_joke_is_a_very_serious/175248.html.

Chapter 9

Introducing Interdependence

INTRODUCTION

Just as every game we play has different rules, there are also diverse dynamics necessary to make our relationships the fulfilling, healthy, and happy ones we dream they will be. Ignorance of these dynamics does not give us a "get out of jail free card." No matter how well-intentioned we are, our lack of knowledge only ensures we suffer for it (see Hos. 4:6). Interdependence is fundamental, scriptural, and creates a win-win scenario for all those wanting healthy relationships. In order to introduce interdependence, we will explore dependence, independence, and codependence.

DEPENDENT

Dependent can be defined as the "relying on someone or something for aid and support." *The American Heritage Dictionary* also defines *dependence* as "the state of being subordinate to, influenced or controlled by something else."[1] Our lives begin with total dependence on others for our survival. We are cared for, nurtured, trained, and instructed by others. It is a natural process of life that we outgrow. Dependence creates a normal and healthy self-centeredness, which is part of an essential carefree childhood. For example, children will want their food immediately and cry for it, whether their caregiver is feeling well or not.

However, when our childish and immature attitudes of self-centeredness and placing all the responsibility for our lives onto others extends into adulthood, all our relationships become dysfunctional. With physical dependence we need someone to do everything physically for us; emotional dependence in an adult means we are dependent on others for our self-worth and self-esteem. There is very little self-reliance or confidence in our own opinion, and we expect others to think and act for us. An emotionally dependent adult is one whose boundaries are confused and enmeshed with others. There is no understanding that their emotions and moods are on "their property," so there is no ownership or responsibility taken for them. This same confusion occurs for many people concerning their dependence on God. As we grow up in our relationship with Him, the Bible teaches us about those things we are clearly responsible for, including working out our own salvation (see Phil. 2:12; Matt 7:7). Blaming God and others for all our disappointments is a sure indication that we are expecting to be absolved of our adult responsibility and wanting to remain dependent.

As adults there are excessive burdens, or "boulders," that become too heavy for us to carry alone as they may crush us. Expecting and needing others to help us with this type of weight, usually during a crisis or tragedy, is not acting dependently or immaturely (see Gal. 6:2). On the other hand, everyone has a load that they need to carry for themselves. The Greek word for *load* in Galatians 6:5 means "cargo or the burden of daily toil"[2] and describes the everyday things that we all need to do. This includes dealing with our own feelings, attitudes, and behaviors, as well as the other responsibilities that God has given to each one of us—even though it takes effort. As opposed to our boulders that are too big to bear, we do have enough strength, resources, and knowledge to carry them.

INDEPENDENT

The dictionary definition of *independent* is "not relying on another or rejecting others' aid or support; refusing to be under the influence or control of others in opinion or conduct; thinking or acting for oneself; not subject to another's authority or jurisdiction; autonomous."[3] The natural, healthy progression of life means that we grow out of dependence and become more and more independent—physically, mentally, emotionally, and financially—until eventually we fully take care of ourselves. It is an indication that we have reached independence when we are directed from within, self-reliant, and able to set limits for ourselves.

We must not confuse independence with defiance. We often comment on a teenager's rebellious stage as them finding their independence, but this is not the same as real independence, which is a vital and healthy step toward maturity and adulthood. Independence is not a reaction to dependence (with dependence meaning others define, control, or misuse their authority), but rather it is a healthy process toward autonomy and self-sufficiency. Steve Covey, in his book *The Seven Habits of Highly Successful People*, says, "If I were physically independent then I would do everything for myself not needing anyone. Mentally, I could think, analyze, organize, process things through for myself. Emotionally, I would be validated from within and I would be directed and disciplined from within. My sense of self-worth would not be a function of being liked or treated well. Independence is obviously much more mature than dependence and is a great achievement in itself but it is not the ultimate success."[4]

He goes on to say that a lot of people will leave their marriages and homes and families all in the name of independence, but this could just be an excuse for forsaking responsibility. "This kind of reaction that results in people 'throwing off their shackles,' becoming 'liberated,' 'asserting themselves,' and 'doing their own thing' often reveals more fundamental dependencies that cannot be run away from because they are internal rather than external. Dependencies such as letting the weaknesses of other people ruin our emotional lives or feeling victimized by people and events out of our control. Of course we may need to change our circumstances. But the dependence problem is a personal maturity issue that has little to do with the circumstances; even with better circumstances, immaturity and dependence often persist."[5]

CODEPENDENCY

Dependent people will either grow into the next stage of independence or get drawn into codependency. The dictionary definition of *codependency* is "a relationship in which a person is controlled or manipulated by another who is affected with a pathological condition."[6] It can also be defined as "people who have let another person's behavior affect him or her, and who is obsessed with controlling that person's behavior." Simply put, codependency can mean living with anyone who requires that you live *their* life and not your own.

The codependency movement was born out of the link between the behavior of those who suffered from alcoholism (the Dependent) and the behavior of those who took care of them. These caregivers (often seen as enablers) would adapt their behavior to take care of the Dependent through means such as overprotection, assumption of responsibility for financial and emotional obligations, lying to cover up drunken behavior, etc. As a result of providing long-term care, these caregivers became overly responsible for their partners, while their own mental and physical health disintegrated. The caregivers were named as "Codependents." After some time, psychologists saw similarities between caregivers of alcoholics and the caregivers of many others who suffered from any pathological condition.[7]

Although the Bible tells us that it is the glory of a man to overlook an offense (see Prov. 19:11), and that love covers a multitude of sins (see 1 Pet. 4:8), this is not to be confused with the codependent relationship, which produces abuse and dysfunction that is soul-destroying for anyone caught up in it. The Bible does not agree with the constant support or denial for those we love that is hurtful, destructive, and sinful. In fact, Galatians 5:19-21 calls such actions "works of the flesh" and those who "practice such things will not inherit the kingdom of God." Our complicity as parent, child, spouse, or friend, no matter how well-meaning, defines us as a codependent.

As many as one-in-four people suffer from codependency, and to a lesser degree, many more. An unhealthy reliance on another person for every thought, action, and feeling means that there will never be the self-definition that maturity brings or God expects. As we become consumed with another's opinion or approval, our individuality becomes lost and we are no longer capable of making our own choices. A person who is codependent is constantly striving to please another person and has made themselves so "self-less" that they lose who they are. This is no sacrifice for the Gospel, the Kingdom of God, or for others, but only a life sacrificed for a significant other who is dysfunctional, abusive, and by fulfilling the lusts of their own flesh, sinful (see 1 John 2:16).

The enemy delights in our confusion concerning these issues, and he deceives many of us into believing that it is the Christian way to allow and support such relationships. The Bible clearly instructs us to "esteem others better than himself" (see Phil. 2:3), but we are also to love ourselves, being good stewards of our time, talents, and treasure. Codependency is not driven by love, but by need, fear, and guilt. We can only be deluded if we think that God sanctions this kind of relationship or any part of it.

INTERDEPENDENCE

The journey of our lives should start with dependence—avoiding codependence—continuing through independence, and finally reaching our destination of interdependence. Whereas independence is a process, interdependence becomes our aim and goal for our relationships. It is defined in the dictionary as those who are "mutually dependent or depending on each other." Romans 12:5 explains this interdependence, when referring to our role within the Body of Christ: "So we, numerous as we are, are one body in Christ (the Messiah) and individually we are parts one of another [**mutually dependent** on one another]" (AMP). First Corinthians 12:25-26 also describes this interdependence, where the apostle Paul uses our bodies as a model for understanding how our lives are interconnected

Although the eye functions independently of the foot, the eye cannot see if the foot will not take it to its destination, and the foot cannot see where it is going without the eye. The eye remains perfectly content to be what it was designed for; never being arrogant or inferior as to what God has made it. In our interdependence, we are neither isolated islands independently doing our own thing, nor are we trying to lose ourselves to another. We are reminded in Psalm 139 to celebrate the unique individuals that God has created us to be, each having distinguished, special, and unusual characteristics and qualities. These are to be discovered and enjoyed, rather than diminished in dependence, lost in codependence, and isolated in independence. The freedom for which we have been set free involves a celebration of all that we are, while encouraging those around us to do the same.

Interdependence is not the completing of one another, as if God made us incomplete or unwhole, but rather it is the completing of all He has called us to do as He intertwines our destinies together. As we realize that even at our very best we cannot achieve or accomplish as much alone, we learn to function as a whole body, all working as God designed us for the greater good. Lives, homes, families, and churches can be built by those who add their value to others, achieving strong and healthy relationships.

To be physically interdependent is to possess a capability and self-reliance without having a reluctance and inability to ask for help when necessary. The emotionally interdependent derive a great sense of self-worth from within, but they also recognize the need for giving and receiving love. These people do not look to others to fill the void that only self-definition and a life lived in God can bring. Limit-setting ensures that our boundaries are in place and protecting us from the bad, while still allowing the good to come in. Steve Covey says, "Interdependence is a choice only independent people can make. Dependent (or codependent) people cannot choose to become interdependent. They don't have the character to do it; they don't own enough of themselves."[9]

The healthy balance between autonomy and togetherness ensures that we have a clearly defined sense of self, while also allowing greater involvement with our loved ones without the risk of losing ourselves in the process. Interdependence helps us achieve the happy and successful relationships we always dreamed of. Ecclesiastes 4: 9-12 talks of freely choosing to add our lives to others:

> *Two are better than one, because they have a good reward for their labour. For if they fall, one will lift up his companion. But woe to him who is alone when he falls, for he has no one to help him up. Again, if two lie down together, they will keep warm; but how can one be warm alone? Though one may be overpowered by another, two can withstand him. And a threefold cord is not quickly broken.*

ENDNOTES

1. http://dictionary.reference.com/browse/dependent.

2. http://bible.org/seriespage/boundary-basics-lesson-1.

3. http://dictionary.reference.com/browse/Independent.

4. Steve Covey, *The Seven Habits of Highly Successful People* (New York, NY: Simon & Schuster, 1989), 50.

5. Ibid.

6. http://dictionary.reference.com/browse/codependency.

7. http://www.buzzle.com/articles/codependent-relationships.html.

8. Steve Covey, *The Seven Habits of Highly Successful People* (New York, NY: Simon & Schuster, 1989), 51.

Chapter 10

Just Jealous

The jealous are troublesome to others,
but a torment to themselves.

–William Penn, 1693[1]

Introduction

We know from Scripture that lucifer was banished from Heaven. He was the most majestic being ever created by God, and he thought he could be like God. He was hurled down before he began causing the destruction of others through this same fleshly passion (see Isa. 14:12). We see this powerful sin in operation from the beginning and throughout the Bible. Cain murders Abel because he is jealous of his success in his workplace and with God (see Gen. 7:4-5). Jacob is jealous of his brother's birthright, steals it, and has to be exiled from his family (see Gen. 25-27). Joseph is hated, almost killed, and eventually sold into slavery because his brothers are jealous of his big dreams and his relationship with their father (see Gen. 37). Saul tries to kill David many times because he is jealous of the popularity that he has won with the people (see 1 Sam. 23). The religious leaders end up crucifying Jesus motivated by pure jealousy because of the power Jesus' displayed and the popularity he received.

These scriptural references warn us to be exceptionally sober and vigilant about this area of our lives, in case we, too, become devoured by it (see 1 Pet. 5:8). This sin has the ability to ensnare us into turning against our friend, hating a brother or sister in Christ, gossiping and slandering family members, and utterly destroying any good and wonderful relationship. We must never minimize its importance as a signal for danger, or be conceited enough to think that it cannot hurt us. It affected many of the great biblical characters, and even Jesus Himself was subjected to it. The devil is out to destroy you, and he will use jealousy to do his bidding; it is really not "just" jealousy!

At times in our lives when we are prospering with whatever we are putting our hands to—enjoying financial blessings, overcoming obstacles, or obtaining the favor of others—we can easily become the target of someone's jealousy. Understanding others' unsolicited antagonism toward us becomes helpful in knowing how to deal with the situation with wisdom and strength. I pray this chapter will especially challenge and encourage you toward God's best for your life.

God's Top Ten

In the Ten Commandments, we are instructed not to covet (see Deut. 5:21). The dictionary explanation of this Old Testament word *covet* is "to have an inordinate and wrongful desire of," and in this we see the beginnings of this sin. Jealousy starts with a wrong desire, one that is totally inappropriate and unwarranted, and says, "I want to have the possessions, the relationships, the status, the talent, and the attention that someone else is having." By this desire, we start our ungodly journey toward the death that all sin produces (see James 1:15). In the English language, envy and jealousy are sometimes used interchangeably, and we see something similar happening with different biblical translations. Lust and covet are also closely linked with envy and jealousy, so we understand they mean very similar things (see 1 Cor. 13:4; James 4:2). They will all *take* at the expense of others—being the opposite of love, which *gives* at the expense of self!

It is significant to note that God is never envious. Nowhere in the Bible can we see that God is envious or that this fleshly impulse should be tolerated or allowed. However, the Bible tells us in Exodus 34:14 that God can be jealous: "You must not worship any other God, for the Lord, whose name is Jealous, is a Jealous God." This jealousy is zealousness, or protective possessiveness, that God has for us. He insists on holding onto the intimate relationship we have with Him through our worship, which is rightfully and exclusively His (see Deut. 5:9 and 6:15). Paul also speaks about this God-kind-of-jealousy in Second Corinthians 11:2: "For I am jealous for you with godly jealousy." Here, Paul is talking about the same zeal to keep God's people at Corinth faithful to their Christian walk when he feared that they were fickle and would stray off the path.

GODLY

Jealousy can, therefore, refer to a proper, balanced, Godly possessiveness with regard to our loved ones or even other things, such as a profession, privileges, treasures, etc. A proper and balanced emotion of jealousy between a husband and wife is watchful and protective, and it is not the same as distrust and suspicion. It causes them not to take each other for granted, but rather put the effort into keeping the relationship healthy. This helps to keep their love alive and intimacy exclusively for each other.

In Romans 11:13-14, the apostle Paul speaks about another positive influence that jealousy might have over us: "I magnify my ministry, **if by any means I may provoke to jealousy** those who are my flesh and save some of them." This kind of stirring or provoking is not rooted in competition, but instead it causes a positive response in us toward God by causing us to "pull up our spiritual socks!" As we see others pressing into their relationship and destiny in God, we can be challenged out of our lukewarmness and apathy and into a more Spirit-filled Christian walk.

UNGODLY

A zeal and rightful possessiveness as laid out above is motivated by love and good intentions. However, James 4:1-3 explains that the only fruit that ungodly jealousy produces is strife, conflicts, and quarrels because its end motive and intent is evil and selfish. This extreme jealousy is an intense and aggressive possessiveness which will suspect unfaithfulness without any truth or evidence. As this kind is driven by fear and reacts to a perceived threat of a valued relationship, it will cause the complete breakdown of trust and anything good in a relationship. More than a breakdown of a relationship, the police in the United States attribute up to 33 percent of all murders committed to this jealousy.[2] The great and wise Solomon described jealousy "as cruel as the grave" (Song of Sol. 8:6), because when the full destructive force of jealousy is released, it will use anger, rage, and violence to achieve its goals. Proverbs 27:4 says, "Wrath is cruel and anger is an overwhelming flood, but who can stand before jealousy" (AMP).

We are naive to think that because we do not manifest rage or violence or are not subjected to it, we have escaped this evil work of the flesh. Church-life provides the perfect greenhouse within which to cultivate this passion. I have found even within my wonderful team of godly ladies who help me run my women's ministry, exactly what the apostle Paul found in Corinth: "envying and jealousy and wrangling and factions" (1 Cor. 3:3 AMP). Just as jealousy successfully breaks down everything good in a relationship, sadly, it has also been allowed to annihilate and devastate all that is good within a team, a church department, and the Church itself. A house quickly gets divided and falls through jealousy (see Matt. 25:12). As long as we are in the process of crucifying the flesh, no one remains immune. As pastor, leader, and mentor, I have learned through costly experience to be a constant watchman for it and to be ruthless in confronting and dealing with it.

This is a small edited excerpt taken from Cyprian of Carthage's treatise[3]:

> *Jealousy is the root of all evils, the fountain of disasters, the nursery of crimes, and the material of transgressions. From it arises hatred and from it precedes animosity. Jealousy inflames greed when those who are wealthier than them can't be content with what they have. Jealousy stirs up ambition when one person sees another more exalted in honors...What a gnawing worm of the soul it is to be jealous of another person's virtue or happiness...To envy his virtue is actually to hate what is admirable in him; to envy his happiness is to hate the blessings God has given him. Either way we are turning the advantages of someone else into our own injury. We are being tormented by the prosperity of someone else, turning their glory into our punishment...If you envy, you're the enemy of no one else's well-being more than your own...Whomever you persecute with jealousy can evade and escape you. But you can't escape yourself. Wherever you may be, your adversary is with you.*

THE WORK OF THE FLESH

From First Corinthians 3:3 and Romans 13:13-14, we understand that both envy and jealousy are a work of the flesh, and that when we are under its control, we are unspiritual and behave like we are unsaved or "mere men." Galatians 5:19-24 explains that when we practice these works of the flesh, we will not inherit the Kingdom of God. However, when we crucify our flesh with its passion, then we may still have a proclivity for something so evil and powerful to continue to take root in our lives. How do we in this regard then "put on the Lord Jesus Christ, and make no provision for the flesh, to fulfill its lusts," as Romans 13:14 instructs?

The fleshly work of jealousy gets its power when we are rooted in insecurity and low self-worth and not in God's Word. Jealousy does not produce insecurity; it merely reveals the rotten roots already there. The fear that we have no value searches for emotional evidence to prove its point, and does so when it sees others being preferred and rewarded more than us. As envy and jealousy make us feel diminished by what someone else has or does, we are to be uprooted out of this old life of inferiorities and be replanted securely on the love of God (see Eph. 3:17). This is the start of our journey out from being a victim of envy and jealousy and into our incredible value as children of God.

The rotten fruit that this work of the flesh has caused in our relationships is endless. This includes the constant need to find "the speck in your brother's eye, but do not consider the plank in your own eye" (Matt. 7:3-5). Further, it has caused us to sorrow at the good fortune and blessings of those around us, rather than celebration, as well as continual dissatisfaction and discontent with our own situation. Blessings, provision, and victories in our own lives become minimized as they come up short to our constant comparisons. Jealousy is poison to a thankful heart.

OVERCOMING THE EVIL HOLD

You are beloved of the Lord and the apple of His eye (see Ps. 17:8). Your worth was established even before you were even magnificently conceived in your mother's womb (see Ps. 139:13). Jesus' death on the cross confirmed how precious and honored you are in His sight (see Isa. 43:4). You are His workmanship (see Eph. 2:10), and His future for you is secure (see Ps. 139:16). Your worth and value is unchangeable, regardless of how you feel and regardless of how talented, successful, good-looking, or anointed anyone else is! If this revelation does not penetrate your heart and become a *rhema* word of God to you, you will always be the victim to these passions and lusts of the flesh. We choose between succumbing to the lies of the devil concerning our worthlessness and responding in hateful slander and strife, and allowing His

Word to renew our mind and responding by walking in and displaying the fruit of the Spirit.

> *But the fruit of the Spirit is love, joy, peace, longsuffering, kindness, goodness, faithfulness, gentleness, self-control. Against such there is no law. And those who are Christ's have crucified the flesh with its passions and desire. If we live in the Spirit, let us also walk in the Spirit"* (Galatians 5:22-25).

It is vital that we remember and meditate on all the words of encouragement that God has spoken over our lives. These reminders of His great plan and purpose for our lives will serve to strengthen and help us to continually crucify the flesh (see Gal. 5:24). Focus on your own individual race—there can be no competitors in your lane—only you can fulfill the unique call on your life. Insecurity and pride are the only results from competing and comparing yourself with others. Jealousy will only slow you down, so throw aside its weight and do not look back or around. Run with endurance the race set before you, always looking to Jesus who is: "the author and finisher of our faith" (Heb. 12:1-2).

ENDNOTES

1. William Penn, *Some Fruits of Solitude*, http://www.quote garden.com/jealousy.html.

2. http://www.americanscientist.org/issues/page2/the-evo-lution-of-jealousy.

3. Philip Schaff, *Treatise 10*, http://www.ccel.org/ccel/schaff/anf05.iv.v.x.html.

Chapter 11

Keys to Kindness

One of the most difficult things to give away is kindness because it keeps coming back to you.

–Cort Flint

INTRODUCTION

We may perceive kindness as a child-like or feminine-type quality. Perhaps our misconception is that kindness is sentimentality for the weak and insincere. However, it is not to be confused with anything other than what the Bible says it is, which is a powerful fruit of the spirit and a desirable and vital asset that should govern our lives and relationships. When we embrace kindness, we become imitators of God Himself.

The Collins English Dictionary defines *kind* as being "friendly, considerate and helpful" and *kindness* as "warm-hearted, pleasant and agreeable." However, in order to understand this word from God's viewpoint, we need to go to its Greek origins. The Greek word is *chrestotes*, meaning "the sympathetic kindliness or sweetness of temper which puts others at their ease, and shrinks from giving pain."[1] This describes a quality or virtue that makes other people feel at ease with us, being assured of our generosity, compassion, and helpfulness; truly, this makes for a vital ingredient for all our relationships.

GOD'S KINDNESS

Kindness is used to describe God Himself more than anyone else in the Bible. However, we seem to forget or underestimate the riches of

His kindness and goodness toward us; it is this kindness that causes the present-day prodigal sons to finally give up their sinful ways and accept God's will for their lives (see Luke 15:11-31). Romans 2:4 says, "Or are you [so blind as to] trifle with and presume upon and despise and underestimate the wealth of His kindness and forbearance and long-suffering patience? Are you unmindful or actually ignorant [of the fact] that God's kindness is intended to lead you to repent (to change your mind and inner man to accept God's will)?" (AMP).

It is helpful to note that whenever the Bible uses the word *good* it is not referring to how morally good God is, but rather how *kind* He is, especially as expressed in His mercies toward us. When the psalmist in Psalm 106:1 refers to God as being good, it is the kindnesses of God that moves his heart, and which should also cause us to worship the Lord. Again, in Psalm 100:4-5, we are called to "Enter His gates with thanksgiving" for the reason "the Lord is good." The Lord our God whom we gladly worship can never divorce Himself from this kindness toward us. It is not only who He is, but also how He relates in commitment and relationship with us: "'For the mountains shall depart and the hills be removed, but My **kindness** shall not depart from you, nor shall My covenant of peace be removed,' says the Lord, who has mercy on you" (Isa. 54:10).

GOVERNED BY KINDNESS

God's expectation of us is to be imitators of Him, treating others with kindness no matter how difficult or ungrateful they are: "**For He is kind** to the unthankful and evil. Therefore be merciful, just as your Father also is merciful" (Luke 6:35-36). Sweetness of temper, or a sweet temperament, is something which is to be cultivated and developed in our lives, just as all the other fruits of the Spirit. It is not something that is gifted us at our natural or spiritual birth, nor is it something we only give to those we like when we feel like it. Galatians 5:21-25 explains that when we have grown this fruit in our lives, we will be living and walking in the Spirit as He intended for us. However, when we are cold-hearted, unfriendly, unhelpful, selfish and rude, or having impatient outbursts, our flesh is not yet crucified and sin still has rule over us (see Rom. 6:11).

Growing the fruits of the Spirit does not happen instantly, but rather it is a process that happens over time. Maximizing the tests and trials God kindly sends our way (often in abundance it feels like) will help us become strengthened and perfected (see James 1:2-4). To test whether we have grown in the fruits like we often think we have, God has devised the offense test to help us. This test allows offenses to rub us up the wrong way, allowing us to see the real person we are beneath our carefully erected facade. This is the same way we can test if something is made of genuine oak wood or if it is just a veneer finish. Since they both look the same on the surface, we need to do a little scratching and testing of our own to immediately reveal its true nature.

Our Christian walk must not be allowed to be unfruitful or barren and should include the kind of growth that Second Peter 1:5-8 talks about:

> *But also for this very reason, giving all diligence, add to your faith virtue, to virtue knowledge, to knowledge self-control, to self-control perseverance, to perseverance godliness, to godliness brotherly kindness, and to brotherly kindness love. For if these things are yours and abound, you will be neither barren nor unfruitful in the knowledge of our Lord Jesus Christ.*

Cultivating a sweet temper and growing the fruit of kindness means we start diligently watching over the words we speak. Jesse Jackson advised, "Never look down on anybody unless you are helping them up." Gossip, slander, and back-biting will cultivate only rotten fruit on our tree. If we are prone to a great deal of conversation, then we must be cautious not to fall into the trouble Proverbs 10:19 warns us of: "In a multitude of words sin is not lacking." It would seem that our young fruit will be prematurely picked off every time we speak unkind, harsh, and judgmental words about someone (see James 3:8-10). We see that the woman in Proverbs 31 set a good example for us by placing a law on her own tongue to make sure that it was governed and ruled by kindness (see Prov. 31:26). As we now are empowered by the Holy Spirit, everything that proceeds out of our mouths must first pass the test of kindness—otherwise it must remain unspoken (see James 1:26). Winston Churchill wisely said, "By swallowing evil words unsaid, no one has ever harmed their stomach."[2]

RELATING TO OTHERS—A BRIDGE BUILDER AND GAP FILLER IN INTERPERSONAL SKILLS

Mark Twain said, "Kindness is the language which the deaf can hear and the blind can see."[3] In relating well to new people, making close friends, and maintaining old relationships, kindness has to be one of our most essential qualities and interpersonal skills. God draws people to Himself through His goodness (see Rom. 2:4), and we too can draw people to us through our kindness. By putting others at ease and being more aware of their feelings and needs than we are of our own, we are displaying this virtue. We are often so wrapped up in our own shyness and insecurities that we don't realize the person sitting right next to us is feeling uneasy and alone.

Isn't it time we got over ourselves and looked beyond our own world and our needs? Kindness is not something we only do in response to someone else's kind act or gesture. It is a quality of our temperament; therefore, it enables us to be kind to the unlovely and unlovable. When we focus on making others around us feel at ease, we will not have enough time to focus on ourselves and our pity parties will have to be cancelled! If only we would realize that our very longing for great and fulfilling relationships starts with us, not others. "Therefore, as the elect of God, holy and beloved, put on tender mercies, **kindness**, humility, meekness, longsuffering" (Col. 3:12). Equipped and armed with this fruit of the Spirit in our life, not only are we acting like God Himself and crucifying the flesh, but we will also start to develop the better, healthier relationships we desire. We will never cease having enough friends because people will be drawn to us, enjoying the ease they feel in our company. William Shakespeare said, "Kindness in women, not their beauteous looks, shall win my love."[4]

KINDNESS SUPPORTS ASSERTIVENESS

Kindness never uses words to sweet talk or puff someone up. Kindness doesn't have hidden motives of wanting to gain something from others. The Bible calls this a lying tongue, which can cause our ruin (see Prov. 26:28), and Proverbs 27:6 says, "Faithful are the wounds of a friend, but the kisses of an enemy are deceitful." Another term used here for flattery is kisses, as they are tantalizing at the time and pleasant to the flesh, but can be deceptive and are to be guarded against. Godly assertiveness on the other hand, which is "speaking the truth in love" as the Ephesians 4:15 instructs, may hurt someone we love, but not harm them. Kindness means that sometimes we might wound someone as we try to help them toward repentance and change. It is never motivated by selfish ambition or a manipulating, corrupt heart, but rather it is compassionate and tender-hearted.

Although kindness shrinks from giving pain and disciplines the tongue so that it does not insensitively hurt people, it doesn't permit passivity. Kindness doesn't negate assertiveness, our boundaries, or our ability to say "no" when someone wants to take advantage of us. The love-walk is godly sacrifice that is given and not taken; thus, we choose to give over and above our means and resources in kindness. If we are unable to be assertive for fear of disapproval, we are deceiving ourselves into thinking we are being kind.

If we cover addictive or destructive behavior of those around us, enabling them to continue in their sin, then we must not imagine that we are being loving or kind. In the same manner, pandering to the insecurities and fears of loved ones is not kindness or love—it is foolishness. As we persevere in God's Word, His truth will set us free to make the necessary adjustments in our life and relationships. Persecution may come from our continued growth into maturity, but walking as Christ did in love and wisdom means that we can be kind and assertive at the same time. We can be self-sacrificing without feeling resentful, and we can say honest and truthful things without malice. "Let all bitterness, wrath, anger, clamor, and evil speaking be put away from you, with all malice. And be **kind** to one another, tenderhearted, forgiving one another, just as God in Christ forgave you" (Eph. 4:31-32).

> *Love suffers long and is **kind**; love does not envy; love does not parade itself, is not puffed up; does not behave rudely, does not seek its own, is not provoked, thinks no evil; does not rejoice in iniquity, but rejoices in the truth; bears all things, believes all things, hopes all things, endures all things. Love never fail* (1 Corinthians 13:4-8).

ENDNOTES

1. http://www.ccel.org/contrib//exec_outlines/fs/fs_13.htm.

2. http://thinkexist.com/quotation/by_swallowing_evil_words_unsaid-no_one_has_ever/219207.html.

3. http://www.brainyquote.com/quotes/quotes/m/marktwain106287.html

4. http://thinkexist.com/quotation/kindness_in_women-not_their_beauteous_looks-shall/146697.html.

Chapter 12

Looking for Love

———◆·❉·◆———

Love is an irresistible desire to be irresistibly desired.

–Robert Frost

INTRODUCTION

When my children were young, I used to help them imagine that within their little tummies was a love tank. This love tank worked very similarly to the other one in their tummies that told them when they were hungry or thirsty. As they would eat or drink something to fill up their food tank, so they could come to me for a cuddle and love when they were feeling a little upset or sad. By doing this, together we could fill their love tank. To this day, my grown daughter still comes to me for these refills. In a very child-like way, I was teaching them that they have love needs, and by recognizing them and asking the right people, they could get these needs filled in the right way. God created us with a human appetite for love and recognition, and whether we are consciously or sub-consciously aware of it, we are looking for others to fill it. This need and longing is both normal and healthy.

LEAKING LOVE TANKS

Due to the sin that first entered the earth through Adam, and the consequent damage that the flesh wreaks, we do not endure our journey through life as God originally intended (see 1 Cor. 15:22). Instead, many of us have ended up with broken and damaged love tanks, its holes cause us to leak out the love we do receive, leaving us constantly feeling inadequate and unloved. Jeremiah 2:13 says, "For My people have committed two evils: they have forsaken Me, the fountain of living waters, and hewn themselves cisterns—broken cisterns that can hold no water." Instead of looking to God, the fountain of Living Waters, we attempt to fix ourselves and fill our needy souls with those things that only cause us more damage. Self-sacrificing behavior such as "keeping the peace at any cost," crossing our own boundaries and consciences to please others, and giving up our own opinions and aspirations for those of others, are just some of the ways we ineffectively try to obtain fulfillment from our relationships.

We may have people who tell us that they love us, but we don't *feel* loved. Maybe we imagine that if they knew who we really were, they wouldn't want to love us. This makes us hide behind a mask and put on a facade of who we think others will love and accept. When our souls are damaged and hurting in this way, our self-esteem and confidence are governed by the opinions of others. Their criticism, disapproval, and unkind words frequently leave us distressed and devastated. Tormented in our thought life, we constantly worry what others think of us, and comparisons always leave us coming up short in our own eyes. Some have even wondered if there will ever be anyone who will love them. These thoughts, beliefs, and behaviors are all indications that our love tank is damaged and running on empty.

The needs of a hungry soul are intense and, left to themselves, will direct us into forming and maintaining destructive relationships. The story of Cain and his brother Abel is a very good warning not to allow perceived rejection to push us into sin and away from the direction that God intended for our lives. Either the Word of God or our sinful broken flesh will rule our every decision, the choice is ours.

> But for Cain and his offering He [God] *had no respect or regard. So Cain was exceedingly angry and indignant, and he looked sad and depressed. And the Lord said to Cain, Why are you angry? And why do you look sad and depressed and dejected? If you do well, will you not be accepted? And if you do not do well, sin crouches at your door; its desire is for you, but you must master it* (Genesis 4:5-7 AMP).

We, too, feel angry, indignant, depressed, and dejected when seemingly unfair and hurtful events take place in our lives. If allowed to control us, these destructive emotions will destroy our relationships like they did for Cain, and we will end up as a wanderer, as well, feeling isolated and disconnected from everyone else.

Looking for Love in All the Wrong Places

Added pressure to feel satisfied and loved comes to the young teenager, and with abusive or neglectful upbringings, they are left without healthy emotions to guide and protect them into loving relationships. Parents, and especially fathers, should be filling up the love tanks for their young daughters and protecting them from the wolves that are plentiful. Unfortunately, some parents go AWOL (Absent Without Official Leave), leaving their children vulnerable and looking to the first person they meet to fill their need for love, approval, and affection. Parents are meant to be God's representative, guarding and governing young lives against the wolves, until they have gained enough wisdom to become self-governing and to discern danger for themselves.

Because the need for love is so compelling, many will "drink" from the wrong places just to feel the smallest amount of significance. Many a young girl has sacrificed her wholeness by giving her body for sex in order to receive a minute amount of love and affirmation. Her life portrays her belief that bad love is better than no love at all. Proverbs 27:7 says, "A satisfied soul loathes the honeycomb, but to a hungry soul every bitter thing is sweet." These encounters add nothing to her heart and only more damage to her already diminished self-respect. Her fantasy, fueled by Hollywood, of a knight in shining armor who rescues her, seldom occurs because she is looking in all the wrong places.

Although we do receive love from people and often feel the love of God through others to us, ultimately, our source must come directly from the Father. We read about this biblical principle of "drinking" and filling our thirsty souls from Heaven, rather than from the world, in the passage where Jesus talks with the Samaritan woman at the well. He tells her that He understands her search for fulfillment via her several lovers (she was onto her sixth). Jesus then offers her the Living Waters by which she will be forever satisfied: "Whoever drinks of this water will thirst again, but whoever drinks of the water that I shall give him will never thirst. But the water that I shall give him will become in him a fountain of water springing up into everlasting life" (John 4:13-15).

Drinking in the Love of God

In Ephesians 3:17-19, the apostle Paul prays one of the most powerful prayers in the Bible. He prays "that Christ may dwell in your hearts through faith; that you, being rooted and grounded in love, may be able to comprehend with all the saints what is the width and length and depth and height—to know the love of Christ which passes knowledge; that you may be filled with all the fullness of God." Webster defines root as "the underground part of a seed plant body, it functions as an organ of absorption, aeration, and food storage or as a means of anchorage and support."[1] The word grounded comes from an architectural term representing a strong foundation.[2]

As Christians, we are to be rooted and grounded in the love of Christ so we may be filled with all the fullness of God (see Eph. 3:17). This means that as we feed upon the Lord, absorbing all of His love into our lives, we will become strongly anchored and supported by the Lord with a sure and solid foundation. The love of God should be the main source from which all our relationships, with others and ourselves, flows. He is the true fountain of Living Waters that Jeremiah 2:13 speaks about, and He will satisfy and fulfill us so we no longer have to look to others to do for us what only the love of God can. We can put our relationships in proper perspective and can give and receive as God intended us to.

GOD IS LOVE

God is eternally of a single mind and purpose, unchanging (see Mal. 3:6). Therefore, if God is love, He is love forever, from before the creation of the world until after the end of time. He is love that never changes; He is not love today and hate tomorrow. He is not love in some situations and apathy in others. He is not love until I disobey Him and then punishment with love forgotten. His character is not dependent on my actions. All of His acts and purposes are consistent with love, as love defines His character: "He who does not love does not know God, for God is love" (1 John 4:8). "And we have known and believed the love that God has for us. God is love, and he who abides in love abides in God, and God in him" (1 John 4:16).

God is everything love is and everything spoken of in First Corinthians 13:4-8. In the verses preceding this passage, we see that the apostle Paul does not say that I must "do" love or "feel" love or "act" lovingly, but rather that I must *"have"* love. This love, God's love, has already been "poured out in our hearts by the Holy Spirit," and therefore if I have God, I have love (Rom. 5:5). My actions will follow to the extent I give God freedom to act in my life. If all my relationships become governed by this love, truly they will be revolutionized forever.

In order to begin manifesting more of this love in our relationships, we must become active in confessing our faith on a daily basis. Meditating and confessing the appropriate Scriptures ourselves is truly a powerful and dynamic way to change the way we think and act. Replacing your name or "I" every time that First Corinthians 13:4-8 says the word *love* is a very good faith exercise for beginners. It looks like this:

> *I am patient and I am kind. I do not envy, I do not boast, I am not proud. I am not rude, I am not self-seeking, I am not easily angered, I do not keep any record of wrongs. I do not delight in evil but I rejoice with the truth. I will always protect, always trust, always hope, and always persevere. When I do these things I will never fail* (NIV).

Here is an additional confession to use as you activate your faith in this area of your life:

> *I boldly confess that God loves me and has revealed His love for me through His Son, Jesus Christ. I know that He has made me His child because He has given me His Holy Spirit, and I now walk in me He does so to help me grow, and so I have no need to fear as He teaches and directs me. I know that it is God Who strengthens, encourages, and equips me for every good work. I put my full confidence in Him, knowing that whatever I ask in the name of Jesus will be done for me. Because of His great love for me I am more than a conqueror in this world, and have an everlasting hope, peace and joy knowing that nothing can separate me from His love.* (John 3:16; Rom. 5:5; 1 John 4:12; 2 Thess. 2:16-17; Rom. 8:37, 39; John 16:26-27).

ENDNOTES

1. http://www.merriam-webster.com/dictionary/Root.

2. http://www.preceptaustin.org/greek_word_studies1.htm.

Chapter 13

Moody or Mature

INTRODUCTION

Definitions of *moody* are "given to gloomy, depressed or sullen moods; ill-humored; expressing or exhibiting sharply varying moods; temperamental."[1] Moodiness means that someone is frequently influenced by bad moods; they are uncertain, unstable, fickle, and volatile. Moodiness is "being irritable or insensitive, given to erratic and unpredictable behavior."[2] Moodiness is not to be confused with sulking, which is only one type of moodiness, not moodiness itself.

All of us have moods, and we cannot be exempt from them. As I say in my first book, *The ABC's of Emotions*, "Many Christians think that their goal is to rid themselves of all negative emotions in order to become more Christ-like. This is neither possible nor healthy. Rather, God requires that we master our emotions and learn to express them in a constructive and righteous way. We do not deny our emotions' existence, but in Christ we deny them the right to rule us. Our goal is to be like Jesus who experienced the full range of human emotion yet did not sin." Moodiness does not exist outside of relationships as it is an inward feeling that is expressed by behavior toward others. In this chapter we look at how to lessen and overcome its negative effect, whether we are the recipient or sender, in order to enhance or even save relationships that are in destructive patterns.

We read in Job 23:13, "But He is unchangeable, and who can turn Him? And what He wants to do, that He does" (AMP). It is comforting and reassuring to know that the God we worship, our Rock, does not lie or change his mind (see Ps. 18:2; Num. 23:19). He is never given to bad or erratic moods, nor is He uncertain, unstable, or fickle (see Mal. 3:6). The character of our heavenly Father is totally dependable, consistent, and predictable, and according to His Word, "with whom there is no variation or shadow of turning" (James 1:17).

MOODINESS IN OUR RELATIONSHIPS

We have said that temperamental people are unpredictable, erratic, and fickle in their behavior. This provides for very little stability for relationships, as it affects everything and everyone in our lives. James 1:8 speaks about the fruit of instability: "[For being as he is] a man of two minds (hesitating, dubious, irresolute), [he is] unstable and unreliable and uncertain about everything [he thinks, feels, decides]" (AMP). People who suffer from moodiness will be like the weather, constantly changing, and those around them never know what season is next. One day they are content and easy going, while the next they are negative, morbid, sulking, or aggressive and generally hard to get along with. This change of mood can many times be attributed to very little, if any, change in their outward circumstances or relationships. We find these kinds of people in our workplaces, our churches, our friends, and families. Where at all possible, it is beneficial to obey the Bible's instruction in Proverbs 24:21(b): "Do not associate with those given to change," as they will constantly make us feel unsafe and unsure.

A moody person plays out their drama using verbal or nonverbal means, with behavior that is outwardly aggressive or more inwardly passive. The end result is the same, however, and that is to let you or others know that their discomfort is paramount. The outward displays include exasperation, frustration, irritation, and anger. Others choose to express their emotions with sarcasm or withdrawal of all communication and affection. Proverbs 12:16 speaks clearly of how God views such a person: "A fool's wrath is known at once, but a prudent man covers shame." There is no gender, age, culture, or temperament bias that lends toward this manner of dealing with life, and all can fall victim to it. The moody person's whole demeanor or countenance speaks loudly, through their pouting, self-pitying, or thunderous looks. They create a heavy atmosphere that is oppressive and clearly felt in the home, workplace, or church, with the message that they are undoubtedly unhappy with the way things and people are around them. Such a person would rather nurture self-pity than resolve the issue.

The saying "rotten roots, rotten fruit" helps us understand that the issue of moodiness goes much deeper than the outward behavior or fruit that we experience. A person ruled by moodiness most likely had a difficult and unhappy upbringing. A simple misunderstanding, accident, or stress caused by others does not produce the appropriate or corresponding response in them. Instead, their frustration and irritation is overwhelming because it is not purely linked to the present—it is connected to an earlier time in their lives. All of us face disappointments that compel us into regrouping, but the person ruled and overcome with their moods is unable to readjust to such setbacks and failings. To this person, their frustration symbolizes something far beyond the present blockage, and they experience it as a warning to react or face intolerable consequences. They feel that if they do not respond by letting others know of their seeming catastrophe, they will be stopped from getting something they vitally need.

It is with this background that the moody person tries to find others to make responsible for their ailments and frustrations. There is usually very little or nothing at all that their victim has to do with their frustration, but the insecure person quickly takes on board the responsibility and blame of such accusations. We come to believe, as does the offender, that we are responsible and able to make their world a better place. The moody person bullies their relationships into compliance, using fear, obligation, and guilt to have everything done their way. Moodiness is, in its essence, manipulating and controlling those around them, who then capitulate in order to keep the peace and avoid punishment. We become pathetically grateful for the "calmer weather" or good moods that come our way, and we are quick to appease, give in, or work harder to keep their approval.

Good moods symbolize the good feelings we long for, such as approval, acceptance, self-worth, and love. However, such good moods are never maintained for long before the next cycle of irritation, frustration, blame, and emotional blackmail begins again. The impossible task of being responsible for someone else's mood will leave all who participate exhausted from constantly walking around on egg shells, producing only resentment and bitterness which will ultimately destroy us (see Heb. 12:15). We cannot repair the past for those we love. We need to withdraw from trying to do so in order for them to assume the rightful ownership of their moods, before the relationship is beyond repair.

MOODINESS IN OURSELVES

Proverbs 25:28 says, "Whoever has no rule over his own spirit is like a city broken down, without walls." Matthew Henry's Commentary adds to the seriousness of this Scripture, "He lies exposed to all temptations of satan and becomes an easy prey."[3] It is time our walls of protection are rebuilt to ensure our victory over the enemy, and knowing where and how we are vulnerable to the attack of the enemy is our first step.

We are three-part beings—spirit, soul, and body—and must not underestimate the profound effect our physical bodies can have on our emotions. For example, many women have already confessed to me that the premenstrual tension that they experience during their hormonal cycle has made them very susceptible to mood swings. My husband, Michael, often teases my daughter and I about this by asking us if our "hors-are-moaning?" Likewise, we must not be surprised if by continual abuse, poor nutrition, and little exercise, we are fatigued, easily stressed, and moody. On one sad occasion, I accidentally put regular gasoline into Michael's diesel truck and found it wouldn't go very far before breaking down! Similarly, overcoming nutritional issues like obesity and a lack of healthy vitamins and minerals will often go a long way to avoiding breakdown and helping us gain victory over constant stress and agitation. "Or do you not know that your body is the temple of the Holy Spirit who is in you, whom you have from God, and you are not your own? For you were bought at a price; therefore glorify God in your body and in your spirit, which are God's" (1 Cor. 6:19-20).

The story of Elijah in First Kings 19:1-8 gives some interesting insights into the truth that physical health is essential to help correct and maintain emotional health. Elijah had been on the run from his enemies for three and a half years before the showdown occurred, when he defied Queen Jezebel and killed all the prophets of Baal in a supernatural show of God's power. Having spent all his energies, Elijah was vulnerable when the final death threat came from the queen. He ran into the wilderness in despair, wanting to give up and die. But in verse 5 of First Kings 19, we see God's answer to his despair, which was first rest and food. Elijah's greatest need at this point was for rest and food, and we only see God dealing with his emotional and spiritual state after his physical health and strength were restored.

MATURITY

As we mature in our understanding of these things (see 1 Cor. 14:20), we embrace the change that we know is inevitable with growth and freedom. Change happens on two levels, one being our inward thoughts and beliefs and the other being our outward behavior. As our minds become renewed, we learn to fully accept ownership of our own moods, understanding that there is no one to blame as the problem and solution lies with us. Likewise, we need to disown the moods of those for whom we have assumed responsibility, placing the load back where the Bible says it should be, on them (see Gal. 6:5). Until this happens inwardly in our thought processes, no outward behavior will be effective (see Rom. 12:2). Read more on this in Chapter 9, Introducing Interdependence.

There may come a time when we will need to assertively speak the truth in love, making it known that we will no longer be the scapegoat of another's moodiness. Giving up our "savior complex" of always trying to fix everything or constantly cheer them up so they are no longer in a bad mood, is relinquishing our past habits and patterns of reacting. At first, changes in our boundaries are hard to implement and difficult for others to accept. With perseverance, however, we will make significant breakthroughs in our relationships. As we persist, and stop rewarding their moody tantrum by pandering to their every whim, there will come a time when we will feel detached and resistant to their moods. This is as essential as ignoring a toddler's tantrum so not to give them the negative attention they are demanding.

If their moods are like our constantly changing weather conditions, we need to become weatherproof and stop being battered and blown all over the place. Our responses, emotions, and actions need to be constant and calm when we deal with them. Learning to give a soft answer "turns away wrath" (Prov. 15:1). When we are different with these people in our lives, we will begin to influence the way they behave and the way they treat us. People only try to manipulate others if they feel they can get away with it and if it will gain them some advantage. Once you have diminished the possibilities of either of these occurring, their behavior has a chance to improve.

Returning to First Kings, we read that as soon as Elijah had rest and food God refocused him on what lay ahead. God never discusses Jezebel again, and she is of such little importance that He sends a servant of a servant of a servant to eventually kill her. He recommissions and directs Elijah for things ahead and wastes no time on the past (see 1 Kings 19:8). Since much of our moodiness is based in our history and not in our present or future, we must strive to shake off the self-pity that tries to strangle us. There will always be people who have had better than us and done worse with it and those who have had worse than us but done better with it. If we see life as being about making us happy, we will despair all the days of our lives. On the other hand, if we understand it is about our training, and therefore our purpose and destiny, then we can do what Romans 5:3-4 instructs: "And not only that, but we also glory in tribulations, knowing that tribulation produces perseverance; and perseverance, character; and character, hope."

Maturity will strive to forget those things that have caused us pain and focus ahead toward all that God has in store for our future:

> *Brethren, I do not count myself to have apprehended; but one thing I do, forgetting those things which are behind and reaching forward to those things which are ahead, I press toward the goal for the prize of the upward call of God in Christ Jesus. Therefore let us, as many as are mature, have this mind; and if in anything you think otherwise, God will reveal even this to you* (Philippians 3:13-15).

ENDNOTES

1. http://dictionary.reference.com/browse/moody.

2. http://www.thefreedictionary.com/moodiness.

3. Matthew Henry, *Matthew Henry Commentary on the Whole Bible* (Peabody, MA: Hendrickson Publishers Inc., 1991), 778.

Chapter 14

Never Say Never

The tongue of the wise uses knowledge rightly, but the mouth of fools pours forth foolishness (Proverbs 15:2).

INTRODUCTION

In a recent "play-fight" between my daughter and her younger brother (who is also much taller and larger than his sister), he overpowered her and laughingly accused her of fighting "just like a girl!" He was teasing her that her fighting skills were inadequate, weak, and possibly even underhanded! All of our relationships will inevitably include conflict and fights. As Jesus said in Luke 17:1, "It is impossible that no offenses should come." There is a war of words that happens around us all the time, and many relationships are fraught with quarrels and strife. Our call as Christians is not never to fight (this is impossible), but rather, as our opening Proverb says, "use knowledge rightly"—or in my kids' analogy, learn how to fight with skill, strength, and character.

The Bible is very clear that we are not to be quarrelsome, argumentative, opinionated, or to seek out fights (see 2 Tim. 2:24; Phil. 2:14). Disagreements, arguments, and upsets are in themselves not destructive, but it is how we choose to deal with them that cause their outcome. Due to poor role models and lack of teaching, we have learned inadequate and ineffective fighting skills. Our emotions are either allowed to run rampant or used to manipulate the conflict, but either way their outcome is destructive. Many times relationships are permanently or irrevocably destroyed, causing pain and hurt and affecting our destinies. Avoidance of difficult issues based on our hurtful past experiences is another inadequate way we try to deal with conflicts. Under the guise of keeping the peace, we give way to the passivity which is motivated by fear, and this only produces a harvest of resentment and dysfunctional relationships. Becoming spiritually minded amidst our relationship conflicts will ensure that their outcomes produce the "life and peace" we are looking for (Rom. 8:6). Let us update our fighting techniques so they are effective and produce an excellent and constructive harvest for us (see Prov. 14:1).

In the heat of a conflict when all we can hear from is our inflamed emotions, it is easy to forget all our good intentions of walking in love and pursuing peace. We tend to react out of old habits and behavior patterns, and all wisdom seems lost or irrelevant. The Bible gives us the keys to how we can overcome this problem. Proverbs 23:7 says, "For as **he thinks** in his heart, so is he." Our thought processes are the starting place for real transformation, and our minds must become renewed to the Word of God (see Rom. 12:2). Our actions and reactions are simply controlled by our emotions, which in turn are controlled by our thought processes and beliefs. In understanding this process, it becomes clear that in order to change our behavior and emotions we must go to the source—our minds. Regular meditation on the Scriptures and understanding what they mean to us in our daily challenges will cause the process of change to transform our lives and relationships. When we start hearing and obeying the Word of God during a heated conflict above that of our fickle emotions, we will truly overcome.

THE FIVE PRINCIPLES OF NEVER SAY NEVER

Before Michael and I had our children, we would self-righteously look at other young children and declare that our children would *never* behave in such a manner. Inevitably, as life has the habit of humbling us all, those behaviors were the exact ones our children would one day display. We quickly learned *never* to say never again. In an attempt to change our thought processes so we do not revert back to old patterns of behavior, we are going to use this phrase "never say never" to help trigger our scriptural memories. The mnemonic of the word *never* gives us five easy principles as to why we must *never* use never in an argument or conflict again:

> N=**Negativity** will make you feel hopeless and defeated.

> E=**Every** subject is thrown into fights and distracts from the real issue.

V=Venting is fleshly and produces death in a relationship.

E=Exaggerations provide no balance.

R=**Rather than resolve** it aims to hurt and to win.

Negativity

Never say *never* in an argument or fight because it makes you feel **negative** and hopeless, and it negates your faith. *Never* makes you feel like you are losing, that it is not worth it, and that you want to give up. Remember that your emotions only respond to what they have been told. So if you believe, think, and use absolute statements like, "You *never* help me" or "You *never* come through for me" or "I always have to do this alone," then your feelings will tell you that you are alone, isolated, abandoned, and defeated. This feeds our ultimate fear that we will be abandoned and unloved. During stressful times of conflict, we may feel these emotions, but to believe that we are in such an unyielding or resolute problem that will never change is painful and destructive.

The truth of God's Word must rule in our minds and take captive the thoughts that are contrary to it (see 2 Cor. 10:5). God's Word tells us we are not alone, abandoned, or left without support or help: "For He Himself has said, 'I will never leave you nor forsake you'" (Heb. 13:5). His Word is full of the victory we need to believe in instead of the defeat and failure we confess when we say "someone or something will *never* change." First John 5:4-5 tells us that we who are born of God are overcomers, and that it is our faith that will give us the victory. Banish the faithless word *never* from your arguments and conflicts, and believe that things can and will change.

Every

Never say *never* in an argument or fight because it throws **every** subject into the argument and distracts from the issue at hand. In our conflicts and disagreements, we like to say things like:

- You *never* support me.

- You *never* do what I want to do.

- You *always* let me down.

- You *always* help everyone else but me.

- You *never* let me know what you are doing.

- You *never* tidy up your room.

This type of language does not keep the issue in the present, but rather it overloads the problem at hand with all other unresolved hurt feelings of the past. In this way, an unimportant or inconsequential disagreement quickly sparks into a bonfire and is much harder to resolve peacefully.

Unfortunately, all of us have past unresolved hurts and issues in our present relationships that have been buried. They become stuffed down, and they want to resurface when we are in a similar situation that triggers those memories. People who are hurting want to hurt others, and they use these feelings as part of their arsenal to hurt and fight back at their opponent—as my daughter was with her brother, they fight underhanded and dirty. These issues do need to be discussed and dealt with, but during another argument is a completely inappropriate and unhelpful time and place to do this. Plan another time that is more suitable and the outcome has a higher chance of bringing peace and resolution. Today's concerns are enough, so stay focused with the present issue at hand. Deal with one problem at a time and you are far more likely to succeed. Removing "never" from our conflicts will alleviate strife and prevent our peace talks from derailing. "A wrathful man stirs up strife, but he who is slow to anger allays contention" (Prov. 15:18).

Venting

Never say *never* in an argument or fight as it gives uncontrolled **vent** to all your emotions. *Never* is theatrical and dramatic. By saying it, we are trying to underline how badly or unfairly we feel we have been treated. It is a classic word used by a self-proclaimed victim with the "poor me" syndrome. Examples include: "God *never* comes through for me," "I *never* get blessed like everyone else," and "I *always* have to struggle more than you." Proverbs 29:11 states, "A fool vents all his feelings, but a wise man holds them back." Venting our hard-done-by feelings makes us difficult to be around and rarely makes us feel any better. It is usually the emotionally charged situations that tempt us to sin in our anger. If we are slow to anger, we remove the fervor that we feel and are no longer a victim to our flesh (see Eph 4:26; James 1:19).

Venting all our feelings, whether in self-pity or anger, allows the tongue to run wildly with no control, causing damage wherever it goes.

James 3:2 states, "For we all often stumble and fall and offend in many things. And if anyone does not offend **in speech** [never says the wrong things], he is a fully developed character and a perfect man, able to control his whole body and to curb his entire nature" (AMP). Name-calling in an argument is another sure indication that our tongue has been released as a fire to cause untold havoc (see James 3:6). Removing the word never from our conflicts helps to rein in the tongue and keep it bridled at all times. As our tongue is reined in, our impulses and feelings will have less means with which to vent themselves, and thus we are able to control our whole body and entire nature.

Exaggerating

Never say *never* in an argument or fight because it is extreme and exaggerates the points. Absolute words like *never* and *always* used in this context in an argument are mostly likely to be a lie. "You *never* help me" or "You *never* clean your room" are most likely untrue. The other person may sometimes help you and on many other occasions do what you have asked from them. In one word—*never*—you are forgetting, ignoring, and misrepresenting the truth. Do not allow your fickle feelings to weigh the situation incorrectly, making an inaccurate judgment: "A FALSE balance and unrighteous dealings are extremely offensive and shamefully sinful to the Lord, but a just weight is His delight" (Prov. 11:1 AMP).

Our tendency to exaggerate in order to win arguments causes us to become unbalanced in our thoughts and emotions and is the very instrument that the devil uses to destroy us (see 1 Pet. 5:8). Well-balanced Christians are temperate, self-controlled, and calm in their emotions, and therefore do not easily fall into the enemy's trap. They are able to experience emotions without being controlled by them. Another attribute of being well-balanced is being assertive. This means we do not conduct our speech with aggression or passivity, but rather we know when to speak up and when to hold back. Those who have practiced this self-control will also be able to take into account the context of the conflict and remember the bigger picture. They are able to remember the many positive qualities of the relationship and not become consumed with only the negative. If we remove never from our conflicts, we are more likely able "to speak the truth in love," as Ephesians 4:15 instructs.

Rather Than Resolve

Never say *never* in an argument as it aims to get "one up" on others and win the argument, rather than resolve the disagreement. "You *never* give as much as I do," "I *never* feel I do enough for you," or "I am *always* the one doing all the hard work" are competitive statements. In the Quarrelsome or Quiet chapter of my first book, *The ABC's of Emotions*, I say this: "The flesh likes to give its own opinion; it wants to be heard; it likes to be right and wants to have the last say. Another word for strife is contention, and the definition of contention is to be in a contest. People will fight to be right." The flesh will always try to use a fight, argument, or disagreement for its own selfish ambitions of proving it is superior—this turns it into a contest.

If it is a contest, the only outcome we must aim for is greater understanding of each other and the peace that has come through adjusting and compromising with those in our lives. Remember "whole people heal people" and never more will you be tested as to your wholeness than during an argument. Be determined to always resolve, compromise, understand another's viewpoint, and ultimately to come to an agreement with them. Be ready to admit, "I think I'm right, but I may be wrong." "But the wisdom that is from above is first pure, then peaceable, gentle, willing to yield, full of mercy and good fruits, without partiality and without hypocrisy. Now the fruit of righteousness is sown in peace by those who make peace" (James 3:17-18).

Chapter 15

Over-the-Top

INTRODUCTION

There is a phrase that I have picked up over the years—OTT or Over-the-Top! Someone or something OTT is over and above the norm, and usually extreme and out of balance. We might say someone's behavior is "So OTT!" In other words, they are unrestrained and excessive in what they are doing. This is, however, not what the Bible calls us to be. In First Peter 5:8, we read that to be OTT in our lives is the devil's playground: "Be **well balanced (temperate, sober of mind)**, be vigilant and cautious at all times; for that enemy of yours, the devil, roams around like a lion roaring [in fierce hunger], seeking someone to seize upon and devour" (AMP). A helpful definition of the word temperate is "moderate or self-restrained; not extreme in opinion or statement; moderate as regards to indulgence of appetite or passion; not excessive in degree as things or qualities."[1]

Living a life of balance is one of the most important qualities I aspire to have in my own life. I have seen too many of God's children become hurt and burned out, and too many relationships destroyed due to excess that causes them to fall into one extreme ditch or the other. Titus 2:3-4 specifically instructs all of us "older" people to mentor and wisely train those younger than us in such qualities as being well-balanced, temperate, moderate, and sober of mind. Titus 2:11-12 then encourages that it will be by His grace, the Holy Spirit's empowering, that we are trained in these qualities giving the devil little means by which to destroy us.

Dr. Edwin Louis Cole said, "Mentally, financially, emotionally, and physically—**balance is the key to life.** Anybody with a checkbook knows

THE A B C 'S OF RELATIONSHIPS

that. Riding a bicycle proves it. Ballast in a ship needs it. A man's mind must have it. Walking requires it. To give balance in life between what is right and what is wrong requires a source greater than self. Real men have God's Word for that source."[2] In adding much more balance to all aspects of our lives and our relationships, we are going to use SOBER as our mnemonic. A definition of sober is "free from excess or extravagance or exaggeration; showing self-control; straightforward; marked by self-restraint and circumspection."[3]

The five principles are:

S=**Over-Sensitive:** Balance in your heart.

O=**Over-Opinionated:** Balance in your speech.

B=**Balance** in your lives.

E=**Over-Emotional:** Balance in your emotions.

R=**Over-Run:** Balance in your activities.

Over-Sensitive

God has blessed us with a sensitivity that was meant to be used for His glory, helping us live our lives before Him and others. A sensitive heart is one that helps us perceive what the will of the Lord is in our lives and gives us a compassionate and forgiving attitude before others' (see Phil. 2:12). Ephesians 4:32 states, "Be gentle with one another, **sensitive.** Forgive one another as quickly and thoroughly as God in Christ forgave you" (TM). To be sensitive to others is a vital relational skill, as it makes us perceptive, responsive, and aware of others' needs and problems. It is also something that we require of others when building relationship with them.

This very blessing, however, becomes a weapon of the enemy when it has been allowed to get out of balance in our lives. Instead of being aware of others like the sensitive person is, the over-sensitive person is only aware and responsive of their own needs, hurts, and upsets, which seem to frequent their lives more often than others. These people have been rooted in rejection so they hear everything incorrectly, colored and misinterpreted by their insecurities. Because their underlying and often subconscious belief is that they are unlovable, they presume and conclude that others will reject and disapprove of them. Pandering to the over-sensitive is hard work, as we have to regularly explain ourselves, our actions, and motives in an attempt to avoid misunderstandings or correct an unintentional offense. Although the Bible calls us to be gentle and insightful of the weaknesses of those around us, the balance of this is that we must not become controlled and manipulated by their intense need for constant sensitivity. These people may need help in overcoming painful heart issues, but they also need to take ownership of their behavior. Doing so is an important part of their healing process.

All of us must exercise self-control over our feelings and actions whenever we understand they are exaggerated, self-indulging, and manipulating. Another way to combat this preoccupation with our insecurities is to become outward-looking and sensitive to the needs of others. Achieving a greater balance of sensitivity to God and others is a great victory for any Christian. We must allow what the enemy meant for harm to bring about good success in our lives, as the tests and trials produce a powerful closeness with God that we may not have experienced before: "And now, isn't it wonderful all the ways in which this distress has goaded you closer to God? You're more alive, more concerned, **more sensitive**, more reverent, more human, more passionate, more responsible" (2 Cor. 7:11 TM).

Over-Opinionated

Achieving balance in our speech can be one of the most powerful tools of any Christian life. The Bible tells us that our speech has such power that it produces the life or death we are experiencing in our present lives (see Prov. 18:21). With our speech, we are able to honor our heavenly Father with praise and thanksgiving while blessing those around us (see James 3:9-12). As His Word lives in our hearts, we are empowered to speak forth wisdom to those we teach and admonish (see Col. 3:16). What a delight it is to provide just the perfect answer at just the right moment for those we love—the Bible says this is priceless! (See Prov. 15:23; 25:11). The right balance of restraint and straightforwardness in our speech stops our "see-sawing" between the one extreme of passivity to the other of aggression. How much healthier our relationships would be if we were able to perfect this area of our lives!

Whenever there is no control or restraint in our speech, the Book of Proverbs calls us a fool. It is not only the quality of what we say—life or death, blessing or curse (see previously mentioned Scriptures)—but also the quantity of our speech that must be restrained. Too many of us talk too much, being quick to reveal our ignorance and immaturity by giving our opinion: "Even a fool is counted wise when he holds his peace; when he shuts his lips, he is considered perceptive" (Prov. 17:28). God has given us one mouth and two ears on purpose. However, instead of being quick to hear and slow to speak as James 1:19 instructs, we are often quick to speak and slow to listen! Many of us would have much less offense and consequent anger in our lives and relationships if we were obedient to the instructions of the first two parts of this Scripture.

In a romantic comedy released a few years ago, one of the characters makes the accurate statement, "Pride is the crutch of the insecure."[4] The urge to speak up often comes from a place of insecurity because we fear being invisible, and pride because we think we know better and deserve to be heard. As we give our opinion, we convince ourselves ("con-our-selves") that they needed to know the truth, or that we were just being honest and real. God, however, calls the same thing opinionated and rude! Romans 12:3 states we are "...not to have an exaggerated opinion of our own importance, but to rate our ability **with sober judgment**" (AMP). If all that is coming out of our mouths is "I think this...or I think that..." then our hearts are overflowing with only ourselves, for it is "out of the abundance of the heart the mouth will speak" (Luke 6:45). Our gossiping tongue is also rooted in our insecurities, as we try to "blow out someone else's candle in order to make ours shine brighter." Insecurity puffs itself up with its own importance in order to hide behind all its feelings of worthlessness and failure. Whatever excuse seems good to us, we will not grow in our walk with God if we continue to justify our undisciplined mouth: "For we all stumble in many things. If anyone does not stumble in word, he is a perfect man, able also to bridle the whole body" (James 3:2).

Balance

First Thessalonians 5:6 instructs us, "be **sober** (calm, collected, and circumspect)" (AMP). The definition of balance is "mental steadiness or emotional stability; habit of calm behavior and judgment."[5] All of our natural lives, whatever we eat and drink, our behavior, mental abilities, heart attitudes, speech, emotions, and spiritual walk, must be governed by a lifestyle of steadiness, stability, and calmness. As we remain teachable to the promptings of the Holy Spirit, He will instruct us in the areas of our lives that are still out of balance. The process of growing the fruit of the Spirit in our lives, such as self-control, is slow and gradual, but diligence and perseverance will ensure they come to full maturity (see Gal. 5:22). As Joyce Meyer often says in her preaching, "We would rather be slow and solid than fast and fragile!"

Over-Emotional

Over-emotional people struggle to live life in the mediocre or beige. It is possible that they have come to perceive the dysfunctional, negative drama of their upbringing and the exaggeration of everything that happens to them as being familiar and normal, while anything calm or temperate is unfamiliar and abnormal. Lack of emotion, or controlled emotion, makes them feel insignificant and invisible. Their self-validation comes from the attention they receive from the drama that they hype up in their lives. They are like an emotional rollercoaster, frequently flying from the chandeliers of life to the depths of difficulties, stress, and blow-ups. The use of emotions to over-dramatize the situation is aimed at evoking or manipulating sympathy and support out of others. They feel justified in being excused from doing tasks, being on time, or being responsible for their lives. Those around them become frustrated with their constant drama and victim mentality. However, any lack of sympathy or support on our part will leave these people feeling offended, falsely accused, and mistreated.

We understand emotions are a blessing from God, created to serve and bless us. Being aware of and expressing these emotions in moderation and restraint makes us human, real, and approachable, which are essential elements in building relationships. Excitement, enthusiasm, and being overjoyed should never be seen as contrary to the Word of God. Remember, we know Jesus was exuberant with His disciples (see Luke 10:21). Without balance, restraint, and moderation, emotions quickly become an enemy that cause havoc and destruction to all our relationships. Excess is the devil's playground, and when our God-given emotions rule over us, we will never enjoy the stability, steadiness, and calmness that should be ours.

Over-Run

"And everyone who competes for the prize **is temperate** in all things" (1 Cor. 9:25). God's best for us is a life that is Spirit-led and purpose-driven. Learning to lead our lives according to His architectural design will be contrary to the direction of our own selfish ambitions, our fickle emotions, and other people's expectations and opinions. A lack of circumspection causes us to not only lose our direction, but also our strength. We must discipline ourselves to be temperate in all the physical and spiritual activities of our lives to ensure that we finish our long distance race with strength. Too many fail to achieve the prize as they have burnt out along the way. William Shakespeare said, "We may outrun by violent swiftness and lose by over-running."[6]

As Christians, we are to become consumed with building the house of God, and constantly laboring in all He has called us to do should be a delight and privilege. However, when we labor and work like it all depends on us, we are falling into the trap that Psalm 127:1-2 speaks about: "Unless the Lord builds the house, they labor in vain who build it; unless the Lord guards the city, the watchman stays awake in vain. It is vain for you to rise up early, to sit up late, to eat the bread of sorrows; for so He gives His beloved sleep." We do labor to build and to guard that which God has given us, but it is all to no avail if we are building and guarding without His master architectural design and direction, or without the strength, peace, and rest He provides. The Bible says "our faith without corresponding works" is dead (James 2:26); in the same theme, "works without the corresponding faith" will be dead because they do not please God. We are saved by His Grace, therefore let us not spend the rest of our Christian walk trying to earn eternity (see Eph. 2:8-9). Galatians 3:3 reminds us, "Are you so foolish? Having begun in the Spirit, are you now being made perfect by the flesh?"

ENDNOTES

1. http://dictionary.reference.com/browse/temperate.

2. http://www.edcole.org/index.php?fuseaction=coleisms. showColeism&id=68&keywords=viewall&page=7&P HPSESSID=71e1d4e7952c0fbc0e3addf5ba1f0a56.

3. http://dictionary.reference.com/browse/sober.

4. Just Married (2003) director Shawn Levy, writer Sam Harper.

5. http://dictionary.reference.com/browse/on+balance.

6. http://www.quotegarden.com/golden-mean.html.

Chapter 16

Prioritizing Prayer

INTRODUCTION

Priority defined means to "give precedence and establish something by importance or urgency; something deserving of prior attention."[1] With so many things deserving our time and attention, it is of the utmost importance we do not allow anything else to usurp the time and place reserved in our lives for prayer. Without the boundary that priorities give our lives, we would be indecisive and aimless concerning our purpose. As the "temple of the Holy Spirit," we are called to be the New Testament "house of prayer" as spoken of in Isaiah 56:7. Prayer involves everything that we do in our heavenly communication with God. It is praise, petitions, confessions, and a partnership with the Holy Spirit. It is the very purpose for which our heavenly Father created us. Adam "walked with God in the cool of the day" (Gen. 3:8), Moses knew Him "face to face" (Exod. 33:11), and Abraham was noted as being a "friend of God" (James 2:23).

A couple of years ago while on vacation with my husband, I heard the voice of God warn me to pray for both our children. It was not that there was anything wrong in their lives at the time, but as they were entering a difficult stage of their teenage years, I knew that the Holy Spirit's unction was for their protection against falling into the enticing ways of the world. My assurance was based on First John 5:14-15: "Now this is the confidence that we have in Him, that if we ask anything according to His will, He hears us. And if we know that He hears us, whatever we ask, we know that we have the petitions that we have asked of Him." God is faithful to do all He has promised us He would do, and today I can testify to His grace and answered prayer in my family's life (see Heb. 10:23).

As we won't do what we don't value, we must come to the revelation that communication with God is one of the greatest pillars upon which we can build our lives. It is through prayer that we can enhance, restore, and protect the relationships that the enemy is intent on destroying (see John 10:10). Tremendous power is made available to us when we subdue the flesh, and with continued and heartfelt prayer, we pray Heaven down into our lives (see James 5:16).

PRAISE

Using Matthew 6:9-13, where Jesus is teaching His disciples to pray, we glean some of the most important principles to ensure that our prayers are powerful and accurately grounded on the Scriptures. In verse 9, Jesus starts with one of the key truths to any heavenly communication with God—praise. "Our Father in heaven, hallowed be Your name." Our entrance into His throne room can be done boldly and confidently, based on the blood of Jesus (see Heb. 10:19). We address our heavenly Father in the name of Jesus, with the praise and adoration due His name, before we make any further petition of Him (see John 16:24). We do not stand shouting to Him in the outer courts, but rather as Psalm 100 tells us, we should "enter His gates with thanksgiving and into His courts with praise."

This priority of magnifying God is a constant reminder to magnify the right things in order to keep our problems in their proper context and proportion. So much time and energy is spent worrying that we act like it is "big problems" and "small God," when it should be "big, magnified God" and "small, insignificant problems." As we come to God celebrating all that He is, we must also believe that He is willing to do as we ask. Hebrews 11:6 instructs us, "But without faith it is impossible to please Him, for he who comes to God must believe that He is, and that He is a rewarder of those who diligently seek Him." James 1:2-8 also sternly admonishes us to believe that God is generous in giving us all we need during difficult and stressful times. He goes on to say that if we doubt God's character and willingness to give us what we need, then we will receive nothing from Him. God will never tempt us with evil, but rather we are to correctly attribute the blame to the desires of our own flesh (see James 1:13-14).

As one of the Hebrew words for worship means "to kiss,"[2] our prayers must always include an intimate affection with our heavenly Father. As we "kiss" Him and receive His absolute love and care for us in return, we are communing with Him just as Adam and Eve did in the Garden. Understanding this giving and receiving of love is an essential building block of a powerful prayer life. The very reason we cast all our anxieties onto Him is because of this tremendous love: "He cares for you affectionately and cares about you watchfully" (1 Pet. 5:7 AMP). Praise and faith rise in our hearts when we start to receive the revelation that our lives are hidden in Him, and that He will never fail or forsake us as He upholds and sustains us through all the tests and trials we find ourselves in (see Ps. 55:22).

PETITIONS

In Matthew 6:10, Jesus instructs His disciples to pray that God's Kingdom come and His will be done on earth. God requires us to pray. He needs us to execute His will and His rulership here on earth because He can only work on our behalf when He is invited. God has chosen to be constrained to His own laws and work through man. We were never called to be gap-finders (fault-finding and gossiping), but rather we are His gap-fillers, interceding to the Father on the behalf of others, just as Jesus presently does for us (see Rom. 8:34).

Matthew 6:11 then teaches us that prayer petitions God for today's "daily bread." God is concerned with the details of our everyday lives and instructs us to present our concerns and requests to Him on a daily basis. Jesus assures us in John 15:7 that these petitions will be answered: "If you abide in Me, and My words abide in you, you will ask what you desire, and it shall be done for you." God not only requires us to petition Him for the people we love and the things we need, but He delights in giving them to us (see John 16:24). Prayer is a daily discipline of asking God for the provision, strength, and wisdom we need for that day. The past is gone and the future is not yet here, but the God who is well-able and willing, will provide us with His fresh manna from Heaven (see Exod. 16:4).

CONFESSION

Matthew 6:12 says, "And forgive us our debts, as we forgive our debtors." Prayer will always include a confession to God of all we need to be cleansed from. As we go to God in prayer with all our concerns of others' wrongful behavior toward us, the Holy Spirit will always first remind us of our own sin. Confession brings His forgiveness which restores our right-standing with Him (see 1 John 1:8-9). God is also acknowledging here the significance of our relationships. Jack Hayford says in his book *Prayer Is Invading the Impossible* that "Jesus prohibits the vertical approach to God that neglects a horizontal approach to people. His insistence is established in words that astonish us with a hard spiritual fact: our being forgiven is contingent upon our forgivingness. Our answers *from* Him depend upon our wills to answer *unto* Him. God refuses to raise a breed of sons and daughters who are unlike Him. He won't allow unforgiveness to continue. It's not in His nature, so He confronts it in ours."[3]

As we need our daily bread of provision, strength, and wisdom, we also need daily confession of our sins and the daily release of all the offenses others have caused us. Such a commitment will ensure that the seeds of bitterness will never find our heart fertile ground within which to take root and cause trouble and defiling of our relationships (see Heb. 12:15). Matthew 5:23-24 clearly confirms this principle that relationship with others takes priority over worship with God: "Therefore if you bring your gift to the altar, and there remember that your brother has something against you, leave your gift there before the altar, and go your way. First be reconciled to your brother, and then come and offer your gift."

Partnership

We have a powerful partnership with the Holy Spirit, who is our prayer enabler. If we are sensitive to Him, He will prompt us in our spirits as for whom and what to pray. This is living the exciting life of the Spirit:

> *Likewise the Spirit also helps in our weaknesses. For we do not know what we should pray for as we ought, but the Spirit Himself makes intercession for us with groanings which cannot be uttered. Now He who searches the hearts knows what the mind of the Spirit is, because He makes intercession for the saints according to the will of God* (Romans 8:26-28).

Such prayers make tremendous power available, dynamic in its working (see James 5:16).

When our dear friends Diana and Graham were struggling with a serious heart condition in their newborn son, I felt Spirit-led not to pray for healing. Instead, as led by the Lord, I prayed that they would get fresh revelation for themselves concerning the promises of God to them as a family. God answered my prayer and they were not only able to find His Word concerning divine healing, but have been able to pray themselves and believe God ever since for the continued health of their now-grown son.

We are to be in perpetual fellowship with God. We are to "live and move and have our being" in Him (Acts 17:28). This means our intercession and prayers for others must be done with all patience and perseverance; never give up praying for those you love. "Praying always with all prayer and supplication in the Spirit, being watchful to this end with all perseverance and supplication for all the saints" (Eph. 6:18). As the apostle Paul prayed unceasingly for those he loved, let us use his prayers to do the same for our relationships:

- Ephesians 1:16-20: "I do not cease to give thanks for you, making mention of you in my prayers: that the God of our Lord Jesus Christ, the Father of glory, may give to you the spirit of wisdom and revelation in the knowledge of Him, the eyes of your understanding being enlightened; that you may know what is the hope of His calling, what are the riches of the glory of His inheritance in the saints, and what is the exceeding greatness of His power toward us who believe, according to the working of His mighty power."

- Colossians 1:9-14: "For this reason we also, since the day we heard it, do not cease to pray for you, and to ask that you may be filled with the knowledge of His will in all wisdom and spiritual understanding; that you may have a walk worthy of the Lord, fully pleasing Him, being fruitful in every good work and increasing in the knowledge of God; strengthened with all might, according to His glorious power, for all patience and longsuffering with joy; giving thanks to the Father who has qualified us to be partakers of the inheritance of the saints in the light. He has delivered us from the power of darkness and conveyed us into the kingdom of the Son of His love, in whom we have redemption through His blood, the forgiveness of sins."

The Lord's Prayer in Matthew 6 ends with verse 13: "And do not lead us into temptation, but deliver us from the evil one. For Yours is the kingdom and the power and the glory forever. Amen." As we find ourselves in a temptation brought on by our own sinful desires (see James 1:13-14), we must pray that God would deliver us. His deliverance is sure, but when and how He chooses to do it is in His hands. So as all prayer should, Jesus ends His prayer with a full surrender to God. Our lives are in His hands, and in Him we put our trust that all things will work out for good (see Rom. 8:28).

ENDNOTES

1.   http://www.thefreedictionary.com/priority.

2.   http://www.jaysnell.org/Articles/kisstoward.htm.

3.   Jack Hayford, *Prayer Is Invading the Impossible* (Alachua, FL: Bridge-Logos, 2002), 128 paraphrased.

Chapter 17

Quality Questions

———◆◆◆◆◆———

An unexamined life is not one worth living.

–Socrates

INTRODUCTION

The definition of a *question* is "a matter for investigation; a subject for dispute; a problem for discussion; a sentence addressed to someone in the interrogative form in order to get information in the reply."[1] In this chapter, we are going to learn why asking quality questions is a good habit and useful skill to learn in order to enhance our relationships. Since the beginning of time, God has asked questions of His people. We see His first question in the Garden of Eden in Genesis 3:19, when God asks Adam, "Where are you?" Of Cain, He asks, "Where is your brother?" (see Gen. 4:9). In the New Testament, we see Jesus continually asking questions of those around Him; for example, He asked the man at the pool of Bethesda, "Are you really serious about getting well?" (see John 5:6), or those who were sick, "What do you want Me to do for you?" (see Mark 10:51).

God does not ask these questions for His information—He already knows the answers—but rather He asks them for our realization and revelation. When Jesus asks the disciples, "Who do people say that I am?" (Mark 8:27), it is Peter who brings forth the revelation. Jesus then explains that it is this significant reply that is to be "the rock upon which He would build His church" (Matt. 16:18). The apostle Paul also needed to receive this kind of revelation, and on the road to Damascus he asks,

"Who are you, Lord?" The Lord answers him, "I am Jesus of Nazareth, whom you are persecuting" (Acts 22:7-8).

Our lives are determined by the quality of our questions. Why should I study this course? Why should I marry this person? How am I adding value to the people around me? Why am I feeling this? Questions like this can help protect us as we search for the root causes of our feelings and issues. Most of us have spent innumerable moments regretting we had not known the truth of a matter. The right questions will help us to avoid these disappointments because they provide us with the complete picture of the situation.

As so many of us have experienced wisdom gained at costly experience, questions help to give us insight in advance rather than in hindsight. They investigate and dispute the issues we are ignorant of and enable us to make better and wiser decisions. We might not have all the answers, but at least our questions are making room for increased understanding. As we are held responsible by God to be a good steward of our hearts and souls, questions are an important tool in the process of self-protection. The generated discussions and disputes that questions provide often arm us with the information we need to avoid the unnecessary hardships of life: "Examine yourselves as to whether you are in the faith. Test yourselves. Do you not know yourselves, that Jesus Christ is in you?" (2 Cor. 13:5).

Quality Questions

We need to learn not only to ask questions, but to ask the *right* questions so that they are not unintelligent or disempowering, leaving us feeling hopeless and despairing. Disempowering questions reinforce negativity; they are accusatory, perpetuate self-pity, and hinder progress. They provide no possibility for quality answers. These questions might include: Why don't they help, understand, or support me? Why do they always (never) do that? What happened to the fun-loving person I knew? What's in it for me anyway? Why can't they be like me? Why can't I do anything right? Why does this always happen to me? How could they be so thoughtless?

Empowering questions, on the other hand, guide us toward hope and direction for our lives. Empowering questions will help us because they:

- Demand answers.

- Stimulate thinking.

- Give us valuable information.

- Put us in the leading position of our own lives.

- Get other people to openly discuss the truth about the relationship.

- Lead to quality listening.

There are many different situations that require us to ask empowering questions, but never more than when it comes to our relationships. As too many of us live life reactively or accidentally, or handle issues as they happen, vital questions can help us focus on what is really important to us. Therefore, what are the quality questions that we need to be asking in our new romantic relationships, our significant relationships, and our relationship with God? Quality questions in relationships need to cover the three aspects of who we are—body, soul, and spirit—as each of these impacts the others. For example, the Bible says "evil company corrupts good habits," and so we see committed Christians aligning themselves with negative relationships (1 Cor. 15:33). This results in their backsliding from God (spirit), which in turn causes stress and strife (soul), and again produces immorality, drunkenness, and fornication (body).

Every person is in a different relational matrix (acquaintance, friend, best friend, engaged, or married), and at each of these levels we need to ask a different set of quality questions. Our expectations of each other will be different for each stage, so we need to start by asking what the expectations are from this relationship and from ourselves. Quality questions also create boundaries to protect us in how much we give and receive from others: Should I be sharing this intimate information with my friend or should I rather be talking to my spouse about it? Should I be counseling and praying with my boyfriend when I am feeling vulnerable to physical temptation? If the right questions aren't asked, the relationship can end in disappointment and breakdown because we have gone too far too fast to build a good foundation. Heart-searching, intimate questions may be difficult as we do not want to face the truths they reveal, but they are intended to protect the treasures of our heart and our God-given relationships.

QUESTIONS TO EMPOWER OUR RELATIONSHIPS

The questions will vary depending on the length or significance of the relationship. For all our new relationships, our starting question must be, "What is the purpose of this relationship?" In the situation where a relationship has the potential for romance, and therefore serious consequences, we need to break it down into the three categories:

- *Spiritual:* Are they spiritually compatible with me? "For what fellowship has righteousness with lawlessness? And what communion has light with darkness?" (2 Cor. 6:14). This needs to broken down even further into what kind of spirituality they have because extensive differences could later cause significant divisions. Do they express and work out their faith in the same zeal and church culture as we do?

- *Soul:* How much do we have in common? Can we become best friends in our relationships through our likes and dislikes, hobbies, and friends? What do they like doing for entertainment and leisure time? I had a friend who only enjoyed sports on a nominal basis, but she married a sports fanatic. The marriage finally deteriorated into a divorce after she found herself alone with their children most weekends.

- *Physical:* Is there a physical attraction? As my previous pastor always used to ask, "Does he make your liver quiver?" How important are looks to us, and what are we expecting from each other in this area? Does our level of health affect the relationship?

Although some of the questions can be adapted to all kinds of relationships, there are several different questions to ask ourselves concerning our significant ones:

- Who am I taking for granted?

- How am I adding value?

- When we were the closest in our relationship, what did we do that we can do again?

- What are the most important emotional needs of my spouse?

- What are their dreams and what can I do to help them come true or move toward them?

- On a scale from one to ten, how do I rate my relationship in terms of the strength and the joy we take in each other?

- Is this rating lower than I'd like it to be?

In asking these empowering questions, we ensure that we are not accommodating any victim mentality in our lives, but actively taking ownership to ensure the success of our relationships.

These questions must clearly examine and judge our own behavior rather than scrutinizing or judging others. Galatians 6:4 says, "But let every person carefully scrutinize and examine and test his own conduct and his own work" (AMP). In Matthew 7:1-5, Jesus gives us a lesson using questions to underline and qualify the point that it is not up to us to judge others, but rather focus on ourselves:

> *Judge not, that you be not be judged. For with what judgment you judge, you will be judged; and with the measure you use, it will be measured back to you. And why do you look at the speck in your brother's eye, but do not consider the plank in your own eye? Or how can you say to your brother, "Let me remove the speck from your eye"; and look, a plank is in your own eye? Hypocrite! First remove the plank from your own eye and then you will see clearly to remove the speck from your brother's eye.*

Questions to Empower Ourselves

In the Gospel of Matthew 6:25-31, Jesus uses this same principle of asking quality questions to reveal to us the uselessness of worry and the care of our heavenly Father. He asks eight questions in only seven verses of Scripture to reveal the truth of verses 32-34:

> *For after all these things the gentiles seek. For your heavenly Father knows that you need all these things. But seek first the kingdom of God and his righteousness, and all these things shall be added to you. Therefore do not worry about tomorrow, for tomorrow will worry about its own things. Sufficient for the day is its own trouble.*

We can evaluate the effectiveness in our social life and in our interactions with others by asking quality questions about our own behavior. If we are unable to objectively answer these, we should enlist a trusted friend who is prepared to speak the truth in love to us. These types of questions will not always bring us easy or complimentary answers, but they will provide us with quality answers that will empower us to change the direction of our lives:

- What kind of first impression do I make?

- Do I smile?

- Am I open or closed in my body language?

- What proportion of time do I listen and talk in a conversation with this person?

- Do I compliment or encourage this person while we are interacting and in the first ten minutes?

- Does this conversation make me sound big and great or build them up and interest them?

- How easy do I make it for people to care for me?

The Holy Spirit encourages, rebukes, and corrects those He loves. Asking the uncomfortable questions keeps us in the center of His will, rather than with formula and duty. These sometimes difficult questions will help us counsel ourselves. They are the tool we need to improve our sense of peace and fulfillment. If, however, they are not providing us with the direction and answers we were looking for, we could try rephrasing them:

- Instead of, What am I getting? ask What am I becoming?

- Instead of, Why is this happening to me? ask Why do I seem to come into situations like this a lot? How can I change my patterns? How can I become better so that I can get to the next level or position that I want to get to? What would I do differently this year if I had no fear? Is my life leading me or am I leading it?

Other empowering questions include:

- Do I really want this?

116

- Will this make my life better or worse?

- Is this taking me closer to where I want to go?

- Is this in line with the dream for my life? Is this the most loving thing I could be doing at this moment?

- What is worth choosing that adds to my life and my character?

"Examine me, O Lord, and prove me; try my mind and my heart" (Ps. 26:2). Let us ask the Holy Spirit to help us gain insight into the direction our relationships are taking. We might not get all the answers we are looking for, but these questions will make room for increased understanding and revelation. We are never to allow them to condemn us, but rather appreciate the help they provide with focusing, making our lives more effective and successful. "There is therefore now no condemnation to those who are in Christ Jesus, who do not walk according to the flesh, but according to the Spirit" (Rom. 8:1).

ENDNOTE

1. http://dictionary.reference.com/browse/question.

Chapter 18

Room for Romance

INTRODUCTION

The dictionary uses many words to describe *romance*: "fanciful; imbued with or dominated by a desire for adventure or chivalry; characterized by a preoccupation with love; displaying or expressing love or strong, passionate and fervent affection."[1] I believe romance is the aroma of life. It is over-and-above the necessity of our relationships; it adds spice and adventure to the mundane, everyday interactions of our relationships; it makes serious reality fun and exciting.

GOD ROMANCES US

God expresses Himself in innumerable fanciful ways. He decorates the earth in unfathomable and indescribable beauty that amazes all humankind. He has created creatures and places in the depths of the oceans that are magnificent, all just to display His extravagant nature. He is passionate and fervent in His love for us and withholds nothing, including His most precious Son Jesus, in order to demonstrate this love (see Rom. 8:32). He is the One who invented romance, this sense of adventure and chivalry, and He takes every opportunity to reveal it to us. First Timothy 6:17 says that God "richly and ceaselessly provides us with everything for [our] enjoyment" (AMP).

Look at these two excerpts from the Song of Solomon, which talk about God as our Lover who desires and delights in us. Such is His love for us that it is as irreversible as death:

- Chapter 2:10: "Rise up, my love, my fair one, and come away!" and verse 14, "O my dove, in the clefts of the rock, in the secret places of the cliff, let me see your face, let me hear your voice; for your voice is sweet, and your face is lovely."

- Chapter 8:6-7: "Set me as a seal upon your heart, as a seal upon your arm; for love is as strong as death, jealousy as cruel as the grave; its flames are flames of fire, a most vehement flame. Many waters cannot quench love, nor can the floods drown it. If a man would give for love all the wealth of his house, it would be utterly despised."

How do we live out our revelation of God's love for us? Do we go to Him out of duty, respect, religious responsibility, and purpose? Or are we constantly flooded with a fresh revelation of how much He pursues us, desiring our presence, attention, and company? God delights being involved in our lives, in all its detail and complexities, and He wants to "quiet us with His love and rejoice over us with singing" (Zeph. 3:17). He lavishes His Love upon us just because He can and just because we are His.

ROMANCING OURSELVES

Making room to spoil and pamper ourselves and bring comfort to our hearts is vital to our emotional well-being. We need to do this in our everyday lives, especially during stressful times. Many times, we feel guilty about doing this as if we don't deserve it, are not worth it, or need someone to tell us to do it. We must make a decision to repair our guilt-reactor, stop playing the victim of our own lives, and enjoy spoiling ourselves. We are worth taking the time, effort, and resources to love on ourselves because we understand its value and importance to our well-being.

As past abuse results in our physical and emotional needs being ignored, we can develop a pattern of not caring for ourselves and not attending to our own needs. We must remember, however, God holds us responsible to look after ourselves, spirit, soul, and body. While His instructions include looking after others, this was never meant to have a detrimental effect on ourselves (see Rom. 12:18; Prov. 3:27). Making ourselves happier will help us to deal better with all the issues presently facing us, making us more content with our relationships. At no greater time are we fulfilling the second greatest commandment that Jesus speaks about in Mark 12:29-31 than when we are doing this: "And the second, like it, is this: **'You shall love your neighbor as yourself.'** There is no other commandment greater than these."

COPING STRATEGIES

Coping strategies are mechanisms we all have and use, whether we are conscious of them or not and whether they are beneficial to us or not. They are automatic responses that help us deal with our present stresses and hardships, as well as all the buried painful memories or stuffed-down emotions. Many times we are not insightful as to what is happening or why we feel compelled to act in a certain way. We should become aware of all of these strategies so that we can minimize the harmful ones and maximize the more beneficial ones. Some examples of the coping mechanisms we use, include: cleaning, sleeping, keeping busy, going out excessively, staying at home excessively, fantasizing or day dreaming, taking medication, drinking alcohol or taking non-prescriptive drugs, smoking, self-harming, withdrawing from people, overeating or starving, working, becoming aggressive, having a bath, painting, writing, phoning someone, walking, having a massage, exercising, dancing, listening to music, talking to someone, reading, etc.

As coping mechanisms are often developed during the difficult times of our lives, we learn to comfort ourselves with negative behavior that creates additional problems for us. Many of these behaviors may start off being harmless, or have limited negative side-effects, but when taken into excess become harmful and destructive to us. Indulging in comfort eating as a means to destress and relax can create weight and health problems that undermine our self-esteem if excessive. Cleaning is a therapeutic exercise which releases tension and gives us a sense of order and achievement, but when we become obsessive with hygiene or cleanliness we can make our families miserable. Sleeping is good and healthy for us as it allows our minds and bodies to relax and revive themselves. Excessive sleeping, however, is harmful to us as it is used to escape our lives. Once awake, we are left feeling overwhelmed and unable to cope with facing realities that may even have worsened due to our absence. Making time and space for ourselves is healthy and beneficial, but if we withdraw excessively, we will become isolated and spiral down into loneliness. Substance abuse, such as alcohol, only has negative and harmful consequences, and it must not be used at all if we are unable to use it in moderation.

Here is a practical exercise to implement: when you are in a good mood, write a list of ten things that you enjoy and bring you pleasure. Then try to do at least one of them a day. For example, pick flowers, go to the movies, do a crossword puzzle or Sudoku, gardening, paint fingernails and toenails, go to bed early, rent a DVD and watch it in bed, make a picnic and go out for the day, go for a walk or swim, buy yourself a magazine or accessory or item of clothing, listen to music, or write. Perhaps we do some of these some of the time, but it is now time to romance and spoil ourselves a lot more.

We may have developed some negative coping skills that are only adding to our present difficulties. It will take time and perseverance not to default to old patterns and habits that have previously had a stronghold over us, but let's decide to start changing our behavior today. We must start with adding more positive and beneficial actions to our lives, including spending time, effort, and resources on spoiling ourselves. First Peter 3:11 instructs us along these lines: "Let him search for peace (harmony; undisturbedness from fears, agitating passions, and moral conflicts) and seek it eagerly. [Do not merely desire peaceful relations with God, with your fellowmen, and with yourself, but pursue, go after them!]" (AMP).

God is certainly our greatest source of comfort, and as we do practical things to pursue peace with ourselves, we understand that it is all the while the "God of all comfort" who will soothe and restore our hurting souls; "Blessed be the God and Father of our Lord Jesus Christ, the Father of mercies and **God of all comfort who comforts us in all our tribulation,** that we may be able to comfort those who are in any trouble, with the comfort with which we ourselves are comforted by God" (2 Cor. 1:3-4).

ROMANCING SPECIAL RELATIONSHIPS

As loving parents we are especially responsible and nurturing of our kids. We may do all the right things that good parents do, but are we truly representative of the Father's extravagant love toward us? Do we spoil and romance our children, not only with our finances, but with the fun, fantasy, and play that their young lives truly revolve around? Or is the love we have for them only expressed in serious responsibilities, discipline, and training? We need to be informed about the seemingly small and insignificant details of their lives, like what their favorite color is and what their fantasies are. We need to learn how to play with them on their level. Be spontaneous and buy small, comical gifts for no reason.

Since our children were 8 years of age my husband Michael has delighted in leaving beautiful Valentine's cards expressing his love for each of them with a red rose (yes, our son too). It is this underserved and unmerited favor that we shower on them that makes them always feel they are so extremely special, valued, and appreciated by us.

I recently wrote a card to my daughter telling her that I adored her simply because she was mine! I adored her before she was born, before she could do anything right or wrong, and I will adore her all the days of my life. I wrote that although there will be times I will either be disappointed or proud of her behavior and accomplishments, this could never subtract or even add to the unconditional love I have for her. Romancing and pampering our children in this manner allows us to have greater insight into just how much our heavenly Father delights in us, His children. His love for us and our children is greater than any human parent can have (see Ps. 27:10). He is never too busy to be thinking of us and searching for ways to show Himself strong on our behalf (see 2 Chron. 16:9).

Never take the special relationships and friendships around you for granted and forget to make room to romance them too. Spoil them with special little surprises and use your creative initiative to make them feel what they truly are to you—loved, special, valued, and appreciated. As I write this book, I daily receive funny, cute, and gorgeous cards, written and sent individually by each member of my Women In Touch team. They tell me that I am appreciated and loved and they are praying for this special book, leaving me thinking how totally spoiled and loved am I!

Romancing Our Life Partners

Watching our worship pastors, Liana and Andrew, romance each other while they were dating, engaged, and newly married was such a delight. Romance, however, should not only be for those who are at this stage of their married lives. It must become something that is built into our intimate relationships as we pamper and spoil each other with all the little gifts, cards, affection, special dinner dates, kind acts, and attention that an "in love" couple does so naturally. As the altruistic and idealistic love gives way to a more mature love, we must remain purpose-driven to romance our partners with our resources, effort, and time, continually sowing seeds of appreciation and value.

It may be hard reviving a relationship that would appear to be roman-tically dead. However, it is important to sow these good seeds, believing that as we add practical actions to our faith, God will restore to us our first love (see James 2:20). I once read of a testimony of a marriage in which the couple were barely talking to, never mind romancing, each other. By faith, the wife started leaving small little surprise gifts and tokens around the house where she knew her husband would find them. Slowly, without much changing at first concerning their verbal communication, he started responding, and over a period of months their relationship was restored to the place of their first love. The destructive cycle was broken and was replaced by a constructive cycle of admiration, pleasure, and gratitude. As we sow romance into our special relationships, whether at this time we feel like it or not, we can believe God for a harvest of a hun-dred-fold return into our lives, producing the great relationships we are believing Him for (see Luke 8:8).

ENDNOTE

1.   http://dictionary.reference.com/browse/romantic.

Chapter 19

Sex, Sex, Sex

INTRODUCTION

Sex was thought up and designed in Heaven by God and given to man before sin entered the human equation. "Then God blessed them, and God said to them, 'Be fruitful and multiply; fill the earth and subdue it'" (Gen. 1:28). In God's blessing, He instructs humankind to procreate by having sex. Our sexuality, which is everything pertaining to our sexual character, is very much part of our humanity and should be celebrated, not denied. Healthy sexuality will be reflected in healthy relationships, but unhealthy sexuality facilitates brokenness, dysfunction, and unhealthy relationships.

HISTORY

History reveals how we got to our present-day thinking in church. Plato first said the body is bad and the soul is good.[1] Augustine, who had sexual baggage in his own life before he became a Christian, dragged some of Plato's writings into his works.[2] Martin Luther did the same thing, and thus the church today perpetuates the underlying attitude that sex is bad and dirty and for procreation only, not for pleasure. The message is that our sexuality and sex itself is something to be ashamed of; furthermore, that sensitive discussions, scriptural teachings, and admonishing of God's people are to be discouraged and frowned upon.

While the world is saying "do it whenever, however, and with whomever," the church is silent, except for a condescending "tutt-tutt." God's people have become naïve and unqualified in understanding themselves, and ineffective in disciplining those in the sexual generation.

Not talking about sex doesn't make us holier or emotionally healthier, rather it leaves people hiding their shame and guilt behind masks as they try and deal with their sexuality and all the related problems—alone.

Statistics tell us that this is a real problem in the world today. For instance, in Britain:[3]

- 72% of British have lost their virginity at age 18 or under.

- The average British person has had 10 sexual partners.

- 80% of men use pornography, with two-thirds doing so at least once a month.

- 42-50% of British couples are unfaithful (this is the highest in Europe).

According to one study, there is a large discrepancy between the attitudes and the actual sexual behavior of teenage girls who are raised in evangelical Christian households. Though the majority say they believe in abstaining from sex until marriage, the average age for first time sex is 16, which is significantly higher than other religious groups.[4]

PROTECTION

Sex, as created by God for His creation, is still good and only produces sin and death where there are no godly restraints or God-given context. The Bible's morality and standards for humankind were only instigated by God for our protection and safe-keeping. If we could envisage a world in which we obeyed God just in this one area called sex, it would be a world without rape, incest, prostitution, pornography, extra-marital affairs, pedophilia, sexually transmitted diseases, and sexual deviations. And it would be a world with much less pain and suffering. Whether we are single or married, our sexuality is something to be celebrated, but also protected.

"You shall walk in all the ways which the Lord your God has commanded you, that you may live and that it may be well with you" (Deut. 5:33). God's instructions must be obeyed if we are to live in this fallen world where mishandling sex damages and enslaves us. God's laws are not petty or irrelevant; they protect us from the unforgiving consequences of sexual sin. God's forgiveness is sure, but many times the consequences of our sin irrevocably affect our lives and those we are in relationship with (see James 1:15). We may jump off a building, regret having done so, repent for this on the way down—although we would have made right with God, the law of gravity would still ensure we see Jesus face to face in Heaven that day!

SALVATION

Salvation is thankfully only our starting block and not our end goal. Getting saved does not automatically sort out our issues, but it does put us into the right position to begin dealing with the issues. The blood of Jesus washes away our guilt, but not our memory, the past, reinforced patterns, or our weaknesses. As our memories are defiled with information we wish we didn't know, and we suffer consequences we wish we didn't need to, we all admit that we would much prefer a convenient, quick, shortcut to the promises of God and overcoming lifestyle. Ultimately, we would prefer not having to learn and use self-control. C.S. Lewis said, "If you think of your life on earth merely for your happiness then soon it becomes intolerable, but if however you think of you life on earth as a place of training and correction then it is not so bad."[5]

If we look through the Bible, we see many great characters suffering due the lack of restraint in their sexuality. Two of these were Samson and David. Samson suffered the consequences of not obeying God in his sexuality and lost his strength, his destiny, and ultimately his life (see Judg. 16:4-22). King David, who was anointed and appointed as king, didn't protect himself from his humanity. Although he had displayed great character throughout his life, he made himself vulnerable to his flesh, gave in to sin, and then had to suffer the consequences of his child's death (see 2 Sam. 12:14). It is encouraging to note, however, that both of these stories do not end with their failure. In his death, Samson accomplishes great purpose and victory over the enemy, and King David goes on to write the great Psalms 51 and 103.

The crown of life that we receive is not about running the faultless race, but rather about enduring temptation, falling down and getting up again, dusting ourselves off and finishing the race (see James 1:12). If we allow God to have the final word in our lives, like Samson and King David, we will always be able to outdo the flesh and the devil. This does not mean that God will take away our struggles; He cannot remove our humanity, nor can we escape the personal responsibility of our souls (see Prov. 4:23). As long as we live in this world, we will continually need to crucify the flesh in order to live overcoming lives (see Phil. 2:12).

FREEDOM

Those who have been caught up in sexual sin find that after salvation they battle to walk righteously before God. Their minds become a battleground, with thoughts of past sin tormenting and dragging them back into their past life. These thoughts become tantalizing and irresistible, but at the same time condemning and despicable to them. At times, we smother that which we previously gave full control, but in moments of weakness or weariness, we give expression to them, feed on them, and become polluted by them. When we finally come to the end of ourselves, we take on board James 5:16. Instead of hiding, covering, and denying our unclean thoughts, we openly confess our struggle to God, being honest enough to admit we love and hate them, and ask for His help. In this place of brutal honesty with God, we confess that although we want what is sinful, we want God more. Amidst the sin drawing us to itself, we hear God calling us; amidst sin desiring to master us, we confess that only God is our Master and our need and desire for Him is greater.

Unclean thoughts try to condemn us, but it is what we do with them that really matters. The defining factor that takes us from defeat to victory is if we care more about what Jesus wants than about what our flesh wants. If this practice does not give longed-awaited release, seeing a trusted confidant or counselor may help with the process. We do not have to pollute someone else's mind with details, but agreement on our freedom from reoccurring thoughts or images will break the stronghold over us. Practice "admitting and submitting" for as often and as long as it takes to procure healing for our defiled, broken, damaged soul.[6]

CLEANSING

We understand that the natural body will smell with all our body odors and that yesterday's shower will not necessarily be sufficient for today. What is true for the physical must also be put into practice spiritually. As we live today in a modern Sodom that is defiled and corrupted by sin that we cannot withdraw from, we come to realize that daily repentance and cleansing with the powerful blood of Jesus is the only thing that works. As we become overcomers in our own lives, so we can become proficient at helping others who are struggling to keep their lives clean.

In John 13, we read the story of Jesus washing His disciples' feet. The culture of His day meant that visitors entered the house with dirty, dusty, and possibly dung-covered feet. The lowest servant or child would then clean the visitor's feet, but in this story we see Jesus doing it. The point He was trying to get across to His disciples was although the world is corrupted and defiled and we have to walk around in it, He is the only One who can really wash it off of us. In John 13:8, Peter reacts indignantly and Jesus rebukes him, not for being dirty, but rather for not wanting Jesus to wash it off: "Peter said to Him, 'You shall never wash my feet!' Jesus answered him, 'If I do not wash you, you have no part with Me.'" If, like Peter, we react and do not want Jesus to cleanse us, then we cannot have any part of Him as we cannot live before Him and in Him with all our unrighteousness.

DRINKING

In Luke 7:48-50, we read about Jesus' encounter with Mary Magdalene, a prostitute, and His loving, forgiving reaction to her: "Then He said to her, 'Your sins are forgiven.' And those who sat at the table with Him began to say to themselves, 'Who is this who even forgives sins?' Then He said to the woman, 'Your faith has saved you. Go in peace.'" God's heart is for those wounded and caught in sexual sin and addictions, and He is quick to forgive those who have faith and confidence in His loving character. C.S. Lewis said, "The human soul has an appetite and it will not stand to be ignored, you will satisfy it rightly or wrongly but it won't go away." People are hungry to feel valuable; and if they don't get it one way, they will try to get it another way.

In John 4:13-15, Jesus meets a Samaritan woman who was living with her fifth sexual partner. Jesus understands her thirst and immediately offers her a living and permanent solution: "Jesus answered and said to her, 'Whoever drinks of this water will thirst again, but whoever drinks of the water that I shall give him will never thirst. But the water that I shall give him will become in him a fountain of water springing up into everlasting life.'" As her God-ordained appetite became misdirected, she was searching for something that her lovers would never be able to give her. As mentioned previously, for many, bad love is better than no love at all, as the Bible explains: "A satisfied soul loathes the honeycomb, but to a hungry soul every bitter thing is sweet" (Prov. 27:7).

Jesus is not only the Living Waters that satisfy our thirst, but also the Bread of Life that will satisfy the most hungry of souls (see John 6:35). If we do not learn to feed and drink from that which God provides, we will feed off something else that will bring dysfunction and death to our lives. This is true for both single and married individuals. Proverbs 5:15-19 admonishes those of us who are married to remain

drinking and feeding off our own spouses; otherwise, we will find ourselves looking elsewhere, drinking from the polluted and toxic, and end
up in sin and destruction.

> *Drink water from your own cistern, and running water from*
> *your own well. Should your fountains be dispersed abroad,*
> *Streams of water in the streets? Let them be only your own,*
> *and not for strangers with you. Let your fountain be blessed,*
> *and rejoice with the wife of your youth. As a loving deer and*
> *a graceful doe, Let her breasts satisfy you at all times; and al-*
> *ways be enraptured with her love.*

ENDNOTES

1. http://webspace.ship.edu/cgboer/athenians.html.

2. http://en.wikipedia.org/wiki/Augustine_of_Hippo.

3. http://observer.guardian.co.uk/sex/story/0,,818356,00.
   html.

4. http://www.newyorker.com/reporting/2008/11/03/
   081103fa_fact_talbot.

5. http://www.allaboutphilosophy.org/cs-lewis-quotes.htm.

6. Sy Rogers online: http://www.youtube.com/watch?v=J2
   LOKpExzZU.

Chapter 20

Twelve Top Tips

---•+••+•---

Introduction

John Maxwell, in his book *The 17 Laws of Teamwork*, was asked what the most important thing to know about leadership is. He replied, "The one thing that there is to know about leadership is that there is more than one thing to know about leadership."[1] Likewise, if I were asked about the one most important thing to know about relationships, I would have to say, "The one most important thing to know about relationships is that there is more than one thing to know about relationships!"

So here are my top twelve tips using the mnemonic of word Relationship:

1. R: Real

2. E: Emotional mastery

3. L: Listen

4. A: Assertive

5. T: Tenacity

6. I: Insight

7. O: Ownership

8. N: Negotiation

9. S: Sowing

10. H: Humor

11. I: Integrity

12. P: Prayer

REAL

Being real and genuine is a vital ingredient for all our relationships. Although we are all on a journey discovering the different facets of who we really are, we must start with what we know is behind the façade or mask. Being aware and accepting of what we feel and think, and then, when appropriate, sharing ourselves, all lead to genuineness. Authentic people are able to be spontaneous in expressing their feelings, and enjoy an openness and transparency in their relationships with the appropriate boundaries. By contrast, an inauthentic person hides his real thoughts, feelings, values, and motives, and cannot risk sharing them. We must dare to be ourselves in order to relate to others. When we become the person we think others want us to be, we lose who we are. The word *personality* comes from the Latin word *persona* which translates as "an actor's mask."[2] Everyone pretends to be something other than what they really are, *some of the time*, as we cannot be self-revealing all of the time. The genuine person however is committed to being the same person inside and out, wherever and with whomever they are with.

EMOTIONAL MASTERY

Our ability—or inability—to control and master our emotions will cause our relationships to be built up or destroyed (see Prov. 14:1). Proverbs 25:28 says, "Whoever has no rule over his own spirit is like a city broken down, without walls." A wise person understands that if they have no self-control over their emotions, they will become easy prey to the enemy who destroys relationships through moodiness, bitterness, manipulation, anger, anxieties, insecurities, jealousies, etc. Our homes should not become war zones ruled by these emotions. In Genesis 4:6-8, we see God warning Cain to rule his emotions of anger, frustration, and resentment so that he might not sin. However, he murders his brother and ends up as a wanderer all the days of his life. If we do not control our emotions, they will control us, destroying our relationships and determining the direction of our lives. The Bible further tells us that it is only in the controlling of our emotions that we attain the spirituality that we desire (see 1 Cor. 3:3).

LISTEN

We will never make or keep the great relationships we desire without the basic, but essential, communication skill of listening. James 1:19 says, "Let every man be swift to hear, slow to speak, slow to wrath." As God has given us two ears and one mouth, we should be listening twice as much as we are speaking. Vanity, which is a constant preoccupation with self, will constantly talk about oneself while hardly ever listening. Nonverbal indications are just as important as verbal ones, and really hearing others will let them know we care about the details of their lives. How many of us have spoken before we have heard the matter and made such a fool of ourselves? (See Proverbs 18:13.) Guarding our mouths and learning to listen more to those around us will enhance and protect all of our relationships by preventing conflicts or helping resolve the ones we find ourselves in. Proverbs 13:3 says, "He who guards his mouth preserves his life, but he who opens wide his lips shall have destruction."

ASSERTIVENESS

Assertiveness is an essential boundary enforcer and relationship builder. It protects us from the extremes of passivity and aggression that destroy relationships. Passivity will cause us to implode with hurt and resentment because we are fearful of standing up for ourselves and expressing our opinion. Aggression is damaging and harmful to others because we express ourselves in uncontrolled emotion of anger, frustrations, and resentments. Assertiveness is the middle road, and as we become more secure, we learn to honestly express what we believe, think, and feel without harming anyone around us. Ephesians 4:15 and 25 underline this principle, instructing us to speak the truth in love. Overcoming the intimidation we feel, and confidently, but calmly, expressing our thoughts and feelings, will facilitate great communication in our relationships. As we do this we are fulfilling Philippians 2:4: "Let each of you look out not only for his own interests, but also for the interests of others."

TENACITY

Possessing a tenacious attitude toward our relationships will ensure that we do not give up on God's blessings. Every relationship takes effort, determination, and perseverance, as all of them *will* suffer difficulties, conflicts, strife, and hardships (see Luke 17:1). Relationships don't just flow or flourish without dedicated, committed effort to build them.

Although many times we may feel like quitting and accepting defeat, it is the tenacious who will not throw away their confidence in God. Hebrews 10:35-36 states, "Therefore do not cast away your confidence, which has great reward. For you have need of endurance, so that after you have done the will of God, you may receive the promise." Every pearl of great price is formed under constant affliction and irritation, as anything worthwhile will not come easily. It is the tenacious who will, through faith and patience, inherit the promises of God for their relationships (see Heb. 6:12).

INSIGHT

Relationships cannot succeed without the self-insight and emotional intelligence of those involved. Psalm 51:6 says, "Behold, You desire truth in the inward parts, and in the hidden part You will make me to know wisdom." God does not want His children ignorant of the emotions, moods, weaknesses, insecurities, and other dynamics that rule our relationships. The apostle Paul pleaded in his letters: "We do not want you to be ignorant..." (1 Thess. 4:13; 2 Cor. 1:8). Several people have invested a great deal in their IQ's (Intelligence Quotient), but have failed to invest in their EQ's (Emotional Quotient), resulting in successful careers and failed relationships. Wisdom, understanding, and knowledge provide us with all we need to build great relationships. If we will meditate and obey Proverbs 24:3-4, we will have good success with all our relationships: "Through skillful and godly Wisdom is a house (a life, a home, a family) built, and by understanding it is established [on a sound and good foundation]; And by knowledge shall its chambers [of every area] be filled with all precious and pleasant riches" (AMP).

OWNERSHIP

Taking responsibility and ownership for our emotions, attitudes, and behaviors is a true sign of maturity and wisdom. Those who do this will not always perceive others to be at fault because they will be able to accurately discern when they are to blame and receive correction for it (see Prov. 9:8-9). Avoidance and denial of our failings and weaknesses, on the other hand, only serve to add more stress to our lives, diminish our self-respect, and damage our relationships. The stewardship of our hearts that God requires, therefore, is ultimately for our protection (see Prov. 4:23). Essential boundaries in relationships cannot be enforced without understanding ownership; we are only responsible for ourselves, not for others. Sometimes the difference between mediocre and great relationships is the ability of both parties to accept ownership for what is rightfully theirs.

NEGOTIATION

Romans 12:16 says, "Readily adjust yourself to [people, things] and give yourselves to humble tasks" (AMP). Negotiation in relationships is the essential ability to compromise and adapt to those around us. We must always be prepared to "yield to reason" as the difficulties and conflicts of relationships confront us (James 3:17). We never compromise on our morals, consciences, boundaries, or anything that would diminish our self-respect, but learning to negotiate the vicissitudes of life and ever-changing relationships is essential in achieving harmony with others (see Rom. 12:16). Harmony implies that like an orchestra with many different instruments and sounds all playing in unison, we are able to produce something heavenly. We have made up a new beatitude: "Blessed are the flexible for they will not break!" We cannot be stubborn, regimented, and unyielding because people are unpredictable and life seldom goes according to our plans. Be prepared to negotiate all the bends in the road up ahead so as to endure and finish the race (see Heb. 12:1).

SOWING

Luke 6:31 sets our golden rule for all relationships, and it follows the simple, irrefutable principle of sowing and reaping: "And just as you want men to do to you, you also do to them likewise." The amount we sow into our relationships is in exact proportion to the amount we will reap (see 2 Cor. 9:6). Whenever we find someone who people love to be around, we will find someone who is rich in mercy and generous with their time, talent, resources, and encouragement. If you are not receiving the attention or appreciation from others that you would like, start to sow these things first (see Gal. 6:7). We must take the focus off ourselves and what we think we deserve and sow generously into the lives of others. This way we will find fulfillment and joy and reap great relationships. Proverbs 18:24 says, "A man who has friends must himself be friendly."

HUMOR

Our relationships should be noted for the constant joy and delight they are to us and others. As Christians, we take ourselves far too seriously and should learn to lighten up and trust God more. Let us become more playful, creative, exciting, and joyful to be around. Making more effort to find fun activities to do together with friends or as a couple or family will deposit great strength into these relationships. Zephaniah 3:17 tells us that God gets exuberant and overjoyed with us His people, and therefore as imitators of God, created in His image and likeness, we are to have fun! Do not settle for boring and lifeless relationships, but believe the Holy Spirit will give you initiative and creative ideas to liven up and enthuse all involved. Excitement often dies between couples when neither make the effort to appreciate and romance each other anymore. Do not wait any longer before you implement your ideas and inject your relationships with a new source of fun and humor.

INTEGRITY

Integrity is a core quality to all relationships and is often only noticed when it is missing. Proverbs 11:3 says, "The integrity of the upright will guide them, but the perversity of the unfaithful will destroy them." Integrity in relationships is the ability to be upright, upfront, truthful, and reliable. Without it, we do not respect those we have relationship with, and they will doubt our validity as a companion or spouse. A lack of integrity makes us unfaithful and untrustworthy in most, if not all, our dealings and will ultimately destroy us. The Bible says that "a house divided against itself will not stand" and in the same way a man or woman divided against themselves will fall (Matt. 12:25). Such people are divided between what they say and what they do. They present one thing on the outside, but are broken and feel something else on the inside—and they struggle with all their relationships (see Prov. 10:9).

PRAYER

Every relationship we have must be bathed in our prayers for protection, favor, and blessing. It must be one of our priorities because we cannot build in the natural without first building in the spiritual. Prayer will give us the advantage over the enemy by helping us discern challenges that may not have occurred yet or receive solutions to those we are already facing. As we go to our heavenly Father with those people we hold dear, we can stand in the gap and fervently intercede on their behalf. At all times and with all kinds of entreaties, we can pray God's will be done in their lives and in our relationship with them. A good example is the apostle Paul who prayed unceasingly for all those he cared about (see Col. 1:9-14; Eph. 1:16-20).

ENDNOTES

1. John Maxwell, *The 17 Indisputable Laws of Teamwork* (Nashville, TN: Thomas Nelson Inc., 2001), xiii.

2. http://encyclopedia.jrank.org/PER_PIG/PERSONAL-ITY_from_lat_persona_or.html.

Chapter 21

Undercover

———◦•⊶•◦———

*But fornication and all uncleanness or covetousness, let it not
even be named among you, as is fitting for saints; neither
filthiness, nor foolish talking, nor coarse jesting, which are
not fitting, but rather giving of thanks. For this you know,
that no fornicator, unclean person, nor covetous man, who is
an idolater, has any inheritance in the kingdom of Christ and
God. Let no one deceive you with empty words, for because
of these things the wrath of God comes upon the sons of disobedience. Therefore do not be partakers with them (Ephesians 5:3-7).*

Introduction

In this chapter, we are going to continue from Chapter 19, Sex, Sex,
Sex, covering challenging subjects that have an enormous effect on our
lives and relationships. These subjects that the church world does not
like to talk about, I call "undercover." We should not be ignorant of
these matters, however, as the Bible says that His people "perish for a
lack of knowledge" (see Hos. 4:6). While God spoke forthrightly to Israel, He was certainly not crass, rude, or unmannerly, and He never
lacked sensitivity or refinement. Although those of this world have
made it a matter of great perversion, we must not react by keeping
silent as if talking defiles us, for it is in this very darkness that the
enemy flourishes.

We can all agree that God must be the most honest, direct, frank,
forthright, truthful, and insightful Person that we know. Unfortunately,

the people of God have become prudish, acting as if they are holier than God. It is our place to speak boldly and wisely about the joy and beauty of sexual intimacy. It is a loving God who not only creates us with these sexual desires, but also gives us the contexts and restraints with which to protect ourselves. Let us not be deceived into minimizing and anaesthetizing ourselves against the reality of what the Bible calls unacceptable sin. God takes sexual sin so seriously that First Corinthians 6:9-11 says those enslaved to it will not inherit the Kingdom of God, or even worse: "Nor let us commit sexual immorality, as some of them did, and in one day twenty-three thousand fell" (1 Cor. 10:8).

ATTRACTION

Wise King Solomon brings us the revelation that we should not "stir up nor awaken love until it pleases" (Song of Sol. 2:7). For those not yet married, the defining question of how far can they go in their physical affections toward the opposite gender is not "where is the line" but rather "when is the time?" In other words, the Bible does not allow sexual contact of any sort before marriage because sexual pleasure is the strictly reserved right of those in a heterosexual, covenantal marriage. Ephesians 5:3 says, "But among you there must not be even a hint of sexual immorality, or of any kind of impurity, or of greed, because these are improper for God's holy people" (NIV). First Corinthians 7:1 and First Timothy 5:1-2 also help us to discern that the godly restraints include no touching of any kind. In judging our actions, we must ask whether we would act in such a manner toward an actual brother or sister? This also helps us to understand that we can build an acceptable non-sexual relationship with other Christians in pursuit of marriage by talking, serving in the house of God together, and in many other forms of relaxation and fun.

As a pastor, I often admonish young couples about the boundaries of their relationship. I am committed to helping them enjoy and protect their God-given relationship. I inform them that although there is a progression of the different levels of friendship as they become more acquainted, there is no progression in physical affection and intimacy. They come to understand that whatever they can do in front of me, holding hands or hugging briefly, etc., they are permitted to do behind closed doors; if they are unable to do what they do openly and in the light, then God will certainly not allow it to be done in secrecy and darkness. Any type of kissing on the lips, touching, and petting is considered by God as foreplay to sex and, without the proper context of marriage, is sinful. If they do not strictly adhere to these physical boundaries placed there by God for their protection, they will fall easily into sexual sin. Although God may be forgiving of these sexual indiscretions, consequences may not be. In our church, we say that the line from the knees-to-the-nose-is-our-no-go-zone! Otherwise, we understand they are trying to usurp the privileges of marriage without any of the sacrifice, commitment, or responsibility.

SATISFACTION

In helping Christians navigate all the complexities of a sexual relationship, First Corinthians 6:12 gives us three criteria with which to rightly divide the word of truth: "All things are lawful for me, but all things are not helpful. All things are lawful for me, but I will not be brought under the power of any." In answering the first two criteria—is it *lawful* (permissible and endorsed by God)—and is it *helpful* in promoting the purpose of marriage, we look at Genesis. Here we see the original pattern for marriage being a gift for one man and one woman to enjoy. Furthermore, God created our bodies for sexual pleasure to be enjoyed in marriage without shame (see Gen. 2:24-25). God has always meant for marriage and sex to be connected and exclusive, and anything other than this is sinful. All sexual activities are to be enjoyed within the freedom and purpose of biblical marital sex. No one purpose should be elevated above the others, but jointly they serve the marriage as God intended:

- Pleasure (Song of Songs)

- Children (Genesis 1:28)

- Oneness (Genesis 2:24)

- Knowledge (Genesis 4:1)

- Protection (1 Corinthians 7:2-5)

- Comfort (2 Samuel 12:24)

In answering the third criteria—is it causing us to be *brought under its power* (is it enslaving or idolatrous)—we look to Romans 12:1. As Christians, we are called to present our bodies as living sacrifices as a spiritual act of worship to God. However, when His people start to worship the creation of the human body rather than the Creator, and they become enslaved to their sexual activities, God views this as idolatrous (see Rom. 1:25). Idolatry is anything that would take pre-eminence and priority over our relationship with God, and Paul makes this connection between sexual sin and idolatry in First Corinthians 10:7-8. It is widely accepted by the medical field that sexual addictions are as addictive, if not more so, than the drug cocaine. The endorphins released are highly addictive and become insatiable and even tormenting, leaving their enslaved always going back to worship at their altar.

"Marriage is honorable among all, and the bed undefiled; but fornicators and adulterers God will judge" (Heb. 13:4). Everything in the marriage bed is acceptable if it has been judged according to each individual couple's consciences and if what the couple enjoy to do is endorsed by God, helpful to their relationship, and not idolatrous. The Bible endorses a variety of sexual activities in the Song of Solomon, including: marital kissing (see Song of Sol. 1:2); a sexually aggressive wife as seen throughout the Song of Solomon; a wife who likes to perform oral sex/fellatio (2:3); masturbation performed on one spouse by another (2:6;5:4-6); massage and petting (4:5); a wife who enjoys her husband performing oral sex (4:12–5:1); a wife who performs a striptease (6:13b–7:9); a husband who enjoys his wife's breasts (7:7-8); erotic conversation (throughout); and ongoing variety and creativity that includes new places and new positions, such as lovemaking outdoors during a warm spring day (7:11-13).

Among this wide range of sexual activities, God never promotes or endorses the use of pornography by a couple in any context. In the New Testament, *porneia* (from which we get the word pornography) is translated as sexual immorality and encompasses all sorts of sexual sins. All pornography creates a lusting after people other than our spouse, and therefore is just as sinful as actual adultery (see Matt. 5:28).

DISTRACTIONS

Christians tend to over-romanticize the wedding vows, leaving them feeling shocked and condemned when they become attracted to someone other than their spouse. It is human to have the capacity and the vulnerability to feel such attractions and desires, whether we are married or single. Just because we love our partner does not make us immune to our senses that are still in operation after we have said our wedding vows. The world will always be full of desirable, good-looking individuals, and integrity is not the absence of attraction, but rather it is the appropriate response to such an attraction. Our vows do not negate our humanity, but by them we commit to staying loyal, faithful, and exclusive. This also demonstrates our love and value for our spouse and reveals our commitment, maturity, and spirituality for God and His Word.

These distractions can occur throughout our married lives and will be temporary as long as we do not feed them or act on them. Many a couple have thought that all their sexual problems would be solved once they were married, but we read that satan only came to tempt Adam after he had a wife (see Gen. 3:6). Many men have simply suppressed their sexuality before marriage, but once they learn how to please a woman and be adventurous within their marriage, their sexual desires awaken full force and the temptation for sin is even increased. As the Bible then admonishes, it is important that such a man discipline himself to channel all his desires onto his wife (see Prov. 5:15-19).

Same-sex attractions happen for both God's men and women. Pretending it does not occur will never make the problem go away, instead it just sends it underground. We all have vulnerabilities, history, memory, and biology, and just because we become born-again does not help us escape our humanity. Many run to God in crisis, expecting that He will help them escape the struggles of their flesh, but such expectations are unrealistic and will be met with disappointment. There are no short-cuts to practicing our God-given authority or to growing the fruit of self-control in our lives to overcome the stronghold of the flesh. We live in a defiled and polluted world, and we must not condemn ourselves for thoughts that exalt themselves against the knowledge of God. We must not give in to, entertain, or act upon them, but rather we are to take authority over them (see 2 Cor. 10:5).

Be diligent to guard against inappropriate emotional intimacy with same-sex friendships as much as with the opposite gender. Overstepping these boundaries can happen to any well-meaning but naive Christian. There is a very real enemy that is scheming to catch us unawares (see 1 Pet. 5:8). We may be more vulnerable to these temptations due to previous abuse that has rendered us thirsty for tender loving care and attention. Some relationally starved people immediately sexualize warm, loving, available contact because they have never known another form of intimacy. Protect yourself and be accountable to others, so if any feelings of attraction occur on either side, they will not be able to go anywhere. It is good to know your strengths, but knowing your weaknesses may determine the difference between life and death.

INFECTION

If a farmer cuts his finger while working with manure on his farm, an infection may set in and affect his whole hand and arm. Likewise, some people who are vulnerable, due to life's many abuses and hardships, may have received such an injury or wound in their soul. As they choose to "sow their wild oats" and end up in sexual sin, which are the "pig sties" of this world, such an injury may become infected with demonic activity, further influencing their lives and causing heartache and misery to all their relationships.

Once the farmer chooses to go to the doctor, the infection could be lanced, the poison removed, and the wound cleansed. The relief from the pain would be instant and life-enhancing. Similarly, a person who has had Jesus set them free from demonic activity experiences this as instant relief and freedom from previous oppression. However, if our same farmer did not bind up his wound correctly but placed his vulnerable hand into the manure once again, another infection would quickly follow, most likely with worse consequences. Likewise, should a person who has been through deliverance of sexual demons return to the filth and defiled areas of this world, the returning torment could be worse. Demonic activity increases when it is able to return and have a greater influence over the once swept clean house (see Luke 11:24-26).

Jesus is well able to set the captives free of demonic activity, especially if they have been deeply bound up by sexual sin and addictions (see Luke 7:50). His blood cleanses us from all unrighteousness (see 1 John 1:9), and washes us whiter than snow (see Ps. 51:7). Be wary, however, of returning to the original sin and place where the infection occurred, lest reinfection causes worse oppression. If we fall short and miss the mark, we must be quick to run *to* Him and not *from* Him, so we may obtain the mercy that we so desperately need and that He so readily provides (see Heb. 4:16). Immediate cleansing and binding of the wound again will ensure no further reinfections occur. The more our minds become renewed to His Word and the more His Word lives and has its permanent home in our hearts, together with the fruit of self-control that begins to rule our responses, the less the enemy and the flesh will be able to influence or determine the outcome of our lives.

Chapter 22

Viewed as Valuable

<hr>

Cheerfulness and contentment are great beautifiers,
and are fatuous preservers of youthful looks.

–Charles Dickens

INTRODUCTION

An extensive American survey asked women, "If you could choose between beauty and brains, which would it be?" By a large majority, most women chose beauty over brains because they saw this as having the greatest value.[1] In this chapter, we are going to look at what we view as having value and how we got these perceptions. These kinds of perceptions, or misperceptions, have a massive impact on our relationships because they are the building blocks of our self-esteem and self-worth. How we see ourselves significantly affects every aspect of how we relate and interact with other people.

There are a variety of fundamental influences, such as culture, which alter our perceptions significantly. For example, there are still many communities today who see a woman's value only in how many sons she can bear and if she is able to keep a home for her family. Our Western world values the clothing size zero of the models and movie stars some worship, resulting in enormous body image distortions among our teenagers. Today's media consists of a billion dollar industry invested in selling us warped and unrealistic images, with magazines airbrushing unachievable perfection into its models. Likewise, television constantly bombards society with its version of what beauty, and in turn, what value is.

Over the past decades while the world was progressively getting more distorted in its views, the church was doing just as badly. Doctrine was widely held that endorsing, encouraging, or enhancing any form of outward beauty, especially in women, was unspiritual, unbiblical, and of the devil. Our worship pastor in church grew up in Romania in strict Christian circles where the practices of wearing no makeup, jewelry, or fine clothing was synonymous with humility and spirituality. As the Body of Christ disqualified itself from being relevant to the younger generation, the devil hijacked the beauty and fashion industry, perverting and distorting all of God's original intent and definition of beauty.

OUR VIEW VERSUS GOD'S VIEW

We need to challenge our perception of how we value ourselves and ask some direct questions:

- What is my value and who or what has defined it for me?

- Who defines my attractiveness?

- What is my body image?

- Do those in my world define how I feel about myself?

- Do the opinions of my past broken relationships still influence the way I feel about myself?

- Is there someone in my world who makes me feel pretty and lovely one day, and ugly, overweight, and stupid the next day?

Such questions are vital in ascertaining if we have allowed other people to have greater power over us than God. Our perception of our worth and value should be based solely upon the Word of God, not such things as our past, our culture, or our relationships. It is time that we bring His beauty back into the church and church back into being beautiful. Churches that are succeeding in bringing the lost back to the fold are being relevant in this way. As God's definition is very different from the world's and the religious system's, we must become very clear and accurate as to whose definition we are aspiring.

Our Bible tells us that God is the Creator, Author, and Inventor of everything that is beautiful:

- Ecclesiastes 3:11: "He has made **everything beautiful** in its time."

146

- Genesis 1:31: "Then God saw everything that He had made, and indeed it was **very good.**"

- Psalm 27:4: "One thing I have desired of the Lord, that will I seek: that I may dwell in the house of the Lord all the days of my life, **to behold the beauty of the Lord,** and to inquire in His temple."

- Psalm 50:2: "Out of Zion, **the perfection of beauty,** God will shine forth."

All the way through the Bible, we see beautiful men and women of God:

- Sarah in Genesis 12:14: "So it was, when Abram came into Egypt, that the Egyptians saw the woman, that she was **very beautiful.**"

- Rachel in Genesis 29:17: Jacob chose and loved Rachel for she was "**beautiful** and attractive."

- Moses in Hebrews 11:23: "By faith Moses, when he was born, was hidden three months by his parents, **because they saw he was a beautiful child.**"

- Queen Esther saves a whole nation against an evil plot to destroy it **because of her beauty** and the favor that God had put on her life (see Esther 2:17).

- Abigail, the wife of Nabal, was a woman of "good understanding and **beautiful appearance**" (1 Sam. 25:3).

We can clearly appreciate that God does not have a problem with beauty! As Christians, we are not of this world, but we are in it; therefore, we live not only before God, but before other people as well (see John 15:19). God gives us human spirits to interact with Him, and our spirits will live on eternally. He also gave us souls and physical bodies to have contact with this natural, physical realm, and God declared them to be "very good" (Gen. 1:31).

TWO TRAPS

It would appear that the family of God is being ensnared by different traps that the enemy sets for us. First, as the world's culture invades the Body of Christ, the outward man is being idolized and God's people are consumed with taking care of it. When we are obsessed and preoccupied with how we look, driven by our insecurities to compare and compete with those around us, we have made for ourselves another god and are worshiping the creature rather than the Creator (see Rom. 1:25). Aspiring to the world's version of beauty can never be attained because it is a lie, and this is not the prize God expects us to aim for. Jesus severely rebukes the religious of His time for being only concerned with their outward appearances: "Woe to you, scribes and Pharisees, hypocrites! For you are like whitewashed tombs **which indeed appear beautiful outwardly, but inside are full of dead men's bones and all uncleanness**" (Matt. 23:27).

Conversely, the church appears to be ensnared by the opposite extreme, making no effort to look after or beautify itself. As poor self-esteem seems to be the greatest culprit, coupled with the false doctrine aligning this with humility and spirituality, God's people—especially His women—have ensured this practice is prevalent in the church world today. Low self-worth and value lie to us and tell us everyone else is more important than we are. We make tremendous effort with our children, spouses, friends, and church because our beliefs confirm they all deserve such attention. On the other hand, we are never able to prioritize our monies and resources to pamper, spoil, and beautify ourselves. If there were a court case made against those treating you badly, I think you might be the first suspect! Those ensnared in this trap have often given up because they do not believe that they are worth it.

God's Way

The world's view is that only "the beautiful" have value. When we believe this, we must beautify ourselves obsessively and worship at the throne of "me." As the outward person is decaying daily, it is a value that is fleeting, unfulfilling, and unreliable. God's way is that we are *beautiful because we have value*, not the other way around. The moment we were thought of by God, we had value. Although our natural parents conceived us, we are made in His image and likeness, and therefore made beautiful. Although our old, stinking mindset might want to deflect this truth, we must allow this report only to define our attractiveness. The devil can make us feel inferior only with our permission.

Let the Word of God have the final say on this matter and do not become discontent and dissatisfied with how God Himself formed and fashioned you. Isaiah 45:9 says that God does not make any mistakes: "Shall the clay say to him who fashions it, what do you think you are making? or, Your work has no handles? Woe to him [who complains against his parents that they have begotten him] who says to a father, what are you begetting? or to a woman, with what are you in travail?

Thus says the Lord, the Holy one of Israel, and its Maker: Would you question Me about things to come concerning My children, and concerning the work of My hands [would you] command Me?" (AMP).

Young girls come to believe that outer attractiveness is the only way to interest a guy, but outside beauty is only skin deep—it is merely the advertising. The greater part of our attractiveness cannot be bought, worn, or applied; the real "drawing" part of us is not the outward person, but the inner person (1 Peter 3:4). Do not be consumed with the mere wrapping paper because the greatest gift and treasure lies within. Awareness of our true worth and value will provide us with a self-confidence that is attractive and irresistible. Someone who is attractive in appearances, but spews forth gossip and slander, is insecure and self-centered and will never be able to exude true beauty. Proverbs 31:30 says, "Charm and grace are deceptive, and beauty is vain [because it is not lasting], but a woman who reverently and worshipfully fears the Lord, she shall be praised!" (AMP).

The outer will never make the inner beautiful, but inner beauty will always exude outwardly, affecting and influencing the outer person. Ultimately, all of us do not want to be loved merely for our outer beauty because this is never who we truly are. We want to be loved with or without make-up, with or without being dressed up and beautified; for it is only then that we truly are valued for all that we are outwardly and inwardly. Our greatest revelation must be that value always precedes beauty. I make myself beautiful because I have value, not to get value.

ADORNING OURSELVES

First Peter 3:3-4 says, "Let not yours be the [**merely**] external adorning with [elaborate] interweaving and knotting of the hair, the wearing of jewelry, or changes of clothes; But let it be the inward adorning and beauty of the hidden person of the heart, with the incorruptible and unfading charm of a gentle and peaceful spirit, which [is not anxious or wrought up, but] is very precious in the sight of God" (AMP). Although we can adorn the outward self, our true priority must always be to beautify our inward person. Therefore, whether we fit into the world's definition of attractiveness or not, our inward peace and assurance comes from the realization that our outward self looks exactly like He designed and purposed it to be to serve His purposes. If He wanted us any different in outward appearances, we would have been born such and so. In all of these matters, it must be God's glory only that we pursue—not other's (see Gal. 1:10).

"For the Lord takes pleasure in His people; He will beautify the humble with salvation" (Ps. 149:4). As we endeavor to remain teachable to all that His Word says we are, the Lord Himself promises to beautify us. True humility is not thinking of ourselves as less than or inferior to what and who He made us, but rather it is accepting all Jesus died to give us. Choosing to no longer accept and agree with other people's opinion of us, or what the media tries to indoctrinate us with, or what our past failures say of us, but choosing to believe what the Word says is true, is being truly humble. We cannot begin to adorn our inner self if we do not accept how uniquely beautiful God has made each of us. It is time we start thinking of ourselves as God does, the apple of His eye (see Ps. 17:8) and truly precious and honored in His sight (see Isa. 43:4). Every time we confess His words over ourselves, we are adorning the inner self.

Our Confession

"I am a beautiful, capable, intelligent, and virtuous woman. I open my mouth in skillful and godly wisdom, and on my tongue is the law of kindness that gives counsel and instruction. I do not eat the bread of idleness or gossip, but choose to speak blessing and God's Word. I will not be discontented or self-pitying about how He has made me, but rather I celebrate that I am fearfully and wonderfully made. I will not seek favor or popularity with others, but I seek first to please my heavenly Father. I know that I am precious and honored in His sight when I trust Him and believe His Word. I accept that I am the apple of His eye and that He takes great delight in me. My steadfast inner strength and peace come from my trust and confidence in God alone. I take care of this, my Temple of the Holy Spirit, but I understand my outside beauty is fading and is not my priority. The charm and grace that exude from my life comes only from a place of inward peace and security with God."

Endnote

1. http://www.reuters.com/article/idUSTRE52N5O9200 90324.

Chapter 23

Wholeness Wins

Introduction

Many people perceive their conflict-ridden relationships as a contest, and they compete to win their arguments and disagreements. However, no one wins in a relationship that is dysfunctional or broken. The only people who always win in all their relationships are those who are emotionally whole. This is because those who are emotionally hurting most likely hurt those around them, while the emotionally whole most likely bring healing to their relationships.

One of the definitions of *wholeness* is "integrity," which in turn means "integrated; together as one person; or an unbroken completeness."[1] When our integrity is intact, we will have a clear, strong value system and moral compass helping to clarify what's right and wrong for us. This is also commonly known as our conscience, which is of vital importance to our relationship with God and others. Acts 24:16 states, "This being so, I myself always strive to have a conscience without offense toward God and men." Those with a clear conscience are able to live before others, without a mask on and enjoying the freedom of being who they are, integrated, and without hypocrisy (see Matt. 23:1-4). It is these people who are able to fulfill the second greatest commandment: "Love your neighbor **as yourself**" (Matt. 23:39). It is through wholeness and self-respect that we first love ourselves, which in turn enables us to love our neighbor and enjoy satisfying and healthy relationships

People have equated integrity with honesty, but it is much more than this. We experience integrity or wholeness as the firm knowledge that "This is who I am, this is what I believe, this is what I am willing to do and this is where I will draw the line." These parameters should anchor and guide us even when we are under pressure, protecting our emotional wholeness. However, a sure sign that we not integrated, but broken within, is when we continually capitulate and compromise on those things we otherwise value and esteem. "And if a house [a home, a family, a life] is divided against itself, that house cannot stand" (Mark 3:25). Each time we override our conscience and become divided against ourselves, we sacrifice the gift that God has given us. The strong foundation that wholeness is meant to provide us becomes eroded away, causing us to be easy targets to control and manipulation. In the children's story of the three little pigs, it is the house that is not built on a solid foundation that the wolf is easily able to blow down with a mere "huff and a puff."

Our DNA

As I mentioned in the very beginning of this book, there are many things in our lives that are optional, but relationships are not one of them. We were created by a relational God who made man in His own image and likeness; therefore, within our very DNA, we have a need for relationships (see Gen. 1:26). In Genesis, we read that although Adam had a perfect environment, a perfect job, and a perfect relationship with his Maker, he still longed for and needed a human companion. Beyond a mere desire, there is within us a need and a longing for physical and emotional intimacy. This need, which is hardwired within our brain's basic genetic structure from birth, is so compelling that even when our relationships are difficult, painful, or frustrating, we still long to belong to someone and to be wanted and cherished for the valued people we are. "What a man desires is unfailing love" (Prov. 19:22).

Also beyond our choice are the homes and environments we are born into. We cannot determine who our parents, siblings, and other family members are and how they will affect our lives. We may not be able to choose whether we participate in relationships we encounter at birth, but we can choose *how* we will contribute to them as adults. This is our only real choice, and we alone have the power to decide whether we will work to make our relationships satisfying and healthy, or to tear them down with our own hands (see Prov. 14:1). Wholeness becomes our choice. The positive insights and changes we make improve all our relationships, simply because all relationships have a similar DNA structure. Let us *choose* to win in all our relationships.

Every relational principle can be found in Genesis. After disobeying God, sin entered the earth and immediately affected Adam and Eve's brand-new, fulfilling, and healthy relationship. The serpent convinced them that God was unjustly trying to withhold something good from them. Once they sinned, their thoughts became flawed with shame. They were overrun with fear, hid from God, and then blamed others (see Gen. 3:10-13). Today these issues still rule and ruin our relationships. Obtaining insight into our fundamentally flawed thoughts—how they produce our emotions and sinful behavior—is vital to living an overcoming life. The devil's scheme to destroy our life by compromising our integrity and overruling our conscience, disrupting our fellowship with God, and destroying all our relationships is no different today from what he did in the Garden with Adam and Eve.

THOUGHTS

"Casting down arguments and every high thing that exalts itself against the knowledge of God, bringing every thought into captivity to the obedience of Christ" (2 Cor. 10:4-6). We have many thought processes that are contrary to the Word of God and beliefs that are still rooted in our past unrenewed minds. In the story of Cain and Abel in Genesis 4:4-8, we see Cain misjudging God's rejection of his offering and believing that God was being unjust and unfair to him. Based on his faulty thinking, Cain experiences anger and jealousy, and in his consequent rage toward his brother, he murders him. When left unchecked or uncontrolled, our emotions will cause us to react in destructive, sinful behavior.

We know that rotten fruit is produced by rotten roots, thus understanding our earliest thought processes is helpful in taking authority over them. "Behold, You desire truth in the inward parts, and in the hidden part You will make me to know wisdom" (Ps. 51:6). Dr. Gary Smalley, in his book *The DNA of Relationships*, states, "If love is given then withdrawn based on performance, we develop a desperate need for someone else's approval. Intellectually we know we cannot please everyone one hundred percent of the time but emotionally we are driven to try!"[2] As children, we make unconscious decisions to never make an angry person angrier, to calm them down for fear they will hurt or leave us. If we take these thought processes into adulthood, we are left with a desperate need to keep the peace together and an inability to express our own anger in a healthy way. None of us likes anger, but if we remain a victim to our thoughts, we will only ever respond to it in unhealthy ways like backing down, placating, or being controlled by it.

If the argument in our mind says we are only acceptable if someone else has approved of us, then we will constantly feel the compulsion to please others. Just as with avoiding anger in unhealthy ways, this belief has the power to cause us to compromise our integrity, override our conscience, and give away our wholeness. We may be competent, rational adults in many other areas of our lives, but we become reduced to a child when someone or something activates hidden thoughts still ruled by of our unrenewed mind. Our thought life is powerful in determining the outcome of our lives: "For as he thinks in his heart, so is he" (Prov. 23:7). We see that renewing our minds to the Word of God will not only transform the way we think, but also how we feel and react (see Heb. 1:3; Rom. 12:2).

FEELINGS

In the story of the talents in Matthew 25:24-25, we see the man with the one talent misjudge the character of His master. His incorrect assumptions cause him to experience fear, which makes him react by burying the talent. His Master is very displeased with him, and the man must suffer the consequences of his sinful, faithless behavior. Our feelings are fickle by nature, and only obey the beliefs and thoughts of our minds. When these are incorrect and unscriptural, we experience fear which causes us to react. Dr. Smalley states that there are many things that we as humans believe we can't live without, and thereby become rooted in several different fears.[3] For example, we may fear losing control or feeling helpless or powerless, so we seize control and threaten to disconnect with others to make them comply. In turn, others fear disconnection or being disliked and rejected, which makes them comply. The cycle repeats—our reaction makes others hurt, which causes them to want us to change, and this pressure makes us react again.

The very need to protect ourselves from having our fear activated makes us vulnerable to those struggling with their own fears, which in turn makes us an easy target for control and manipulation. Dr. Smalley suggests that all our deepest desires and fears stem from the need for connection and control. Women most likely have a core fear related to loss of relationship, not being heard, and not being valued. Most men, on the other hand, have a core fear of helplessness or feeling controlled; they fear failure or getting stepped on. Some version of these two core fears exists in all of us, and although the Bible tells us not to fear, we must understand how we tend to react in order to empower our relationships.

"Though I walk through the valley of the shadow of death, I will fear no evil; for You are with me; Your rod and staff, they comfort me" (Ps. 23).

REACTIONS

Dr. Smalley states, "We tend to react, consciously or unconsciously, in well-worn patterns."[4] For example, when we fear losing a relationship, we may subconsciously end up suffocating it in an attempt to overcome our feelings of helplessness. Or when someone hurts us and our fears of loss are triggered, we may end up acting in destructive manipulative ways in an attempt to hold onto the relationship. So although our thoughts and emotions are our starting point, it is the consequential behavioral patterns that end up sabotaging our relationships. Our knee-jerk reactions ensure that the promise of healthy, intimate relationships never becomes realized in our lives.

Both Adam and Eve did not accept responsibility, but rather played the blame game that many still tend to do today (see Gen. 3:10-13). We must, however, accurately divide this ownership and not assume too little (as Adam or Eve did), but neither must we accept the responsibility of other people's lives. In many homes, children are made to be the parents or adults, coming to believe that their parents lives depend solely on them. This is not only overwhelming to children, but also teaches them to be responsible for others when they should not be. As we take the correct weight of responsibility, we remain compassionate without renouncing our own physical and emotional well-being for the sake of others.

God has made us the captain of our souls, and although we are meant to be submissive to those He has put over us, He is not pleased when we hand over our responsibility to another (see 1 Pet. 5:5). Again, this may be rooted in childhood experiences where the authority figures always knew best. Subconsciously, we believe that these idealized beings are smarter, wiser, and more "right" than we are, and so we react by abdicating our God-given stewardship over our own souls. Here are some good statements to make concerning our wholeness and accepting the rightful ownership of our souls:

- I take a stand for what I believe in, and I listen to my conscience.

- I don't let fear run my life.

- I confront people who have injured me.

- I define who I am rather than being defined by other people.

- I keep promises I make to myself.

- I protect my physical and emotional health.

- I don't betray other people.

- I tell the truth.

ENDNOTES

1. http://www.dictionary.net/integrity.

2. Dr. Gary Smalley, *The DNA of Relationships* (Smalley Publishing Group, 2007).

3. Ibid., 28 para.

4. Ibid., 8 para.

Chapter 24

Xplain Not Excuse

———————

An excuse is worse and more terrible than a lie;
for an excuse is a lie guarded.

–Alexander Pope[1]

INTRODUCTION

The dictionary defines *excuse* as "to seek to remove the blame of; to justify; to release from an obligation or duty; to seek exemption; a pretext or subterfuge." Unfortunately, justification, rationalizing, covering, and lying have become a way of life for many. Our sin nature finds the world of excuses, half-truths, and blame-shifting early on in our lives and becomes a professional at it, easily maintaining it throughout our lives. This "excuse culture" is prevalent in the church where the enemy has confused God's people, making them feel guilty when they hold people to account for their attitudes and behavior. Christ-like behavior promotes striving for excellence and greatness in all that we are and do, as we see Jesus doing this in the Gospels (see 1 Pet. 2:9 AMP).

Right from the Garden of Eden, and throughout the Bible, humankind has not wanted to accept responsibility for sinful behavior. In Genesis 4:4-10, we see Cain blaming God and his brother for having not done well with his offering. The Lord's answer is simple: "So the Lord said to Cain, 'Why are you angry? And why has your countenance fallen? If you do well, will you not be accepted? And if you do not do well, sin lies at the door. And its desire is for you, but you should rule over it.'" The words do well here carry with them the concept of being successful and happy by doing the right thing.[2] The opposite is

157

also true—when we don't do the right thing, we will have problems and will not be happy or successful.

EXCUSES

Lying

Excuses are used to cover or hide the true reason behind behavior; they are plain lies. Lying is accomplished by either avoiding the truth or not telling the whole truth. As God is a God of truth, He does not allow us to get away with lying: "Therefore, putting away lying, 'Let each one of you speak truth with his neighbor,' for we are members of one another" (Eph. 4:25-26). Excuses are also used to cover up other lies. When someone uses an excuse, that person is hoping that it will help to free or exempt him or her from some obligation or duty. For example, when someone says, "I'm sorry I'm late but I got stuck in traffic," they may or may not have been stuck in traffic. Maybe they did not leave early enough, had a late start, or didn't take into account the expected or unexpected traffic congestion. Not wanting to accept that we have treated others badly by disrespecting those who were waiting for us, we give excuses. The person feels that their excuse has now exempted them from the duty or work that they were not keen on doing.

Pain

Bob Philips, in his book *Controlling Your Emotions*, says that "excuses are an attempt to avoid facing the reality of uncomfortable feelings or unpleasant circumstances."[3] Our pride will make use of excuses to help to cover our failings and weaknesses. The statement, "I just don't understand computers; I'll leave that to younger people; after all, you can't teach an old dog new tricks," may mean we are too undisciplined to learn, take a new course, or read a book—a truth that is much harder to accept. We may cover our embarrassment and feelings of inadequacy by offering ourselves an excuse or cop-out. It is usually our need to cover a fear that brings an excuse to mind because it helps us avoid an accusation or criticism. Standing on other people's toes or touching a sensitive subject will usually produce an excuse because people's frail egos do not want to cope with the truth. When anxious over a confrontation, fearful of embarrassment, or threatened by a punishment, we most likely take the easiest route by giving an excuse. Frank Crane said, "Responsibility is the thing people dread most of all. Yet it is the only thing in the world that develops us, gives us manhood or womanhood."4

Guilt

Excuses help us to justify and rationalize our sinful attitude or behavior. Justification with God means "just as if I have never sinned," but when we justify ourselves, we are trying to exempt ourselves from all discipline and the consequences that our sin brings. A guilty party will spend a lot of energy trying to convince others that their actions and attitudes are warranted and necessary, and many times they believe these same lies.

> *He will punish sin wherever it is found. He will punish the heathen when they sin, even though they never had God's written laws, for down in their hearts they know right from wrong. God's laws are written within them; **their own conscience accuses them, or sometimes excuses them.** And God will punish the Jews for sinning because they have His written laws but don't obey them. They know what is right but don't do it* (Romans 2:12-16 TLB).

Often we have a guilty complex because we are guilty. If we faced the truth, we would know:

- We are not being kind or loving to our family.

- We are being rude and impatient.

- We are putting off doing necessary chores around the house.

- We are not helping with the housework.

- We are exceeding the speed limit.

- We are making personal phone calls on work time.

- We are exaggerating and spreading gossip.

- We know we have not been studying for our tests.

- We are not being honest with our income tax.

- We have not helped a tired friend.

- We have flirted with those of the opposite sex.

- We have shouted too much at the kids and punished them unfairly.

This list can go on indefinitely. Our still small voice of conscience prompts us with the guilt we feel when we know we have done something wrong, but we do not want to own up to it. If we admitted we were wrong, we would have to take responsibility, give up our excuses, and do something different. We would have to do things right or well, as Cain needed to! "This being so, I myself always strive to have a conscience without offense toward God and men" (Acts 24:16).

MANIPULATION

Excuses mask true motivation, as our reasoning and arguments are designed to confuse, deceive, and manipulate. We may use different tactics:

- *Drama* aims at changing the subject so that the listener will forget the original question or observation. For example, if the question is, Why didn't you show up for the meeting, we were really counting on your help? The answer may be, I would have been there but George called, and did you know that George lost his job and his wife is in the hospital having an operation? In a few clever maneuvers, the question was evaded and the pressure relieved.

- *Helplessness* maximizes the victim mode to get a person off the hook. For example, "I can't help it, you don't know what I have to put up with, and if you had as many problems as me then you would also react."

- *Aggression:* Instead of defensive mode, they immediately attack back, acting as if you are questioning their character and motives. These are the people who pride themselves on their logical thinking, will believe their own excuses, and get angry when anyone challenges them. They cannot accept that their excuse is being questioned, and react as if someone is attacking their deductive reasoning abilities and their integrity.

- *Anger:* Hostility and an outburst of temper will help keep most people from questioning them. Anger helps them get their own way because others back off to keep the peace.

As such, they train those around them not to question them any further.

BLAME

Erica Jong said, "Take your life in your own hands, and what happens? A terrible thing: no one is to blame."[5] In First Samuel 15:17-26, Saul excuses his disobedience with a but: "**But** I have obeyed...", "**But** the people...." Although he finally confesses his sin of wanting the people's approval above God's, he still does not want to face the consequences of his behavior. In verses 25 and 26, we see it is too little too late: "'Now therefore, please pardon my sin, and return with me, that I may worship the Lord.' But Samuel said to Saul, 'I will not return with you, for you have rejected the word of the Lord, and the Lord has rejected you from being king over Israel.'"

I say we are to "get our big *buts* out of the way!" Our "buts" will always blame others! If we find ourselves apologizing with a big "but" at the end of our apology, then be assured we are not truly sorry and have not taken our due responsibility. We most likely have found someone or something to use as our scapegoat; "prove" it was not our fault. Just like King Saul, we are still justifying why we can't obey God. A scapegoat gives us someone or something to defer to, rather than having to be mature adults responsible for ourselves. Such immaturity and foolishness is still acceptable in a child, but we are to put away all childish things and grow up into all things as God requires (see 1 Cor. 13:11). It rarely our physical age that matures us, rather it is our ability to accept responsibility.

EXPLANATIONS

A definition of *explanation* is "a statement made to clarify something and make it understandable; a meaning or interpretation; actions or motives with a view to adjusting a misunderstanding or reconciling differences."[6] Whereas excuses damage our relationships with lies, pain, guilt, manipulation, and blame, explanations promote understanding, wisdom, communication, compassion, and growth in our personal lives and relationships.

- *Understanding:* Psalm 51:6 says, "Behold, You desire truth in the inward parts, and in the hidden part You will make me to know wisdom." Explanations are our allies because they help us understand how we got to the place of sin and brokenness. Understanding is the doorway to our deliverance. Explanations do not absolve the person from guilt that comes from wrong doing, but they act to clear up misunderstandings.

- *Wisdom:* Explanations help us to understand the journey we have been on so that we do not repeat the same mistakes again. It is foolishness not to learn from the past, but we are bound to repeat it if we do not examine what happened and why. This can be our greatest source of wisdom even though it was gained at costly experience.

- *Communication:* Explanations are an essential part of communication. When we do something that may cause hurt or when we bring correction and discipline to those submitted to us, an explanation is helpful and beneficial. Let us not confuse this with the need to please by explaining ourselves to everyone even those we are not accountable to.

- *Compassion:* Explanations facilitate reconciliation because they explain how misunderstandings or conflict originated. Explanations accept responsibility and do not excuse negative behavior, thus apologies are most likely to occur.

- *Growth:* Explanations encourage personal growth and maturity. Bob Phillips says, "Mental, emotional, and spiritual growth come from facing problems rather than running from them. It involves struggle, pain and courage. It requires exercise of the will and the determination to not give up. Out of the battles and conflicts of life our spirit and character are molded. When we accept responsibility for our own actions and attitudes, we grow toward maturity. We gain self-respect and begin to adjust to the pain that is common to all people."[7]

TO CONCLUDE

Excuses for our failure, our choices in life, and our bad decisions fuel our negative victim attitudes and sinful behavior. Making excuses instead of taking 100 percent responsibility for our lives is the hallmark of people who fail to succeed. Let us not minimize their destructiveness, as they allow us to continue in dysfunction, carnality and sin, ensuring that we stagnate emotionally and damage all our relationships. By not facing and speaking the truth, we are trying to evade our God-given responsibility with dire consequences. No one can live our lives for us, only we are in charge. There may be events that occurred to us as children that we can do nothing about; however, we must have the courage to take on those things we can do something about.

Remember, explanations are beneficial as long as there is no big "but" at the end of them. Let us take action today and become aware of each and every excuse that would first form in our minds. Once identified, take authority over them so that they do not find their way into our emotions or behavior: "For the weapons of our warfare are not carnal but mighty in God for pulling down strongholds, casting down arguments and every high thing that exalts itself against the knowledge of God, bringing every thought into captivity to the obedience of Christ" (2 Cor. 10:4-5).

ENDNOTES

1. Alexander Pope cited in http://www.tentmaker.org/Quotes/ excuses_failure_quotes.html.

2. Bob Philips, *Controlling your Emotions* (Eugene, OR:Harvest House Publishers, 1995), 135.

3. Ibid., 137 paraphrased.

4. Frank Crane cited in http://www.saidwhat.co.uk/topic-quote/responsibility.

5. Erica Jong cited in http://www.quotationspage.com/quote/27142.html.

6. http://dictionary.reference.com/browse/explanation.

7. Bob Philips, *Controlling your Emotions* (Eugene, OR:Harvest House Publishers, 1995), 31.

Chapter 25

Yes to Youthfulness

———◦◦◦———

You are as young as your faith, as old as your doubt;
as young as your self-confidence, as old as your fear;
as young as your hope, as old as your despair. In the
central place of every heart there is a recording chamber.
So long as it receives messages of beauty, hope,
cheer and courage, so long are you young.

–General Douglas MacArthur

INTRODUCTION

We were uniquely and extraordinarily designed by our heavenly Creator to have three parts: spirit, soul, and body, divisible only by the Word of God (see Heb. 4:12). We are a spirit, we have a soul, and we live in a body—this is the simplest way to explain this mystery. First Thessalonians 5:23 identifies these separate parts: "Now may the God of peace Himself sanctify you completely; and may your whole spirit, soul, and body be preserved blameless at the coming of our Lord Jesus Christ." In the greatest commandment given to humankind, we understand that God requires we love Him with all of our being: "And you shall love the Lord your God with all your heart, with all your soul, with all your mind, and with all your strength" (Mark 12:29-31). If we worship God just with our spirits and our souls, but we do not engage our bodies, we are not fully obeying this commandment.

These three different aspects affect each other constantly. For example, when we start exercising, our physical bodies complain loudly to our souls to stop this perceived punishment. There are other times when our spirit will instruct our soul, as we see David do so: "Why are you cast down, O my soul? And why are you disquieted within me? Hope in God, for I shall yet praise Him for the help of His countenance" (Ps. 42:5). Someone who is mature in God has their mind renewed to His Word, and will only allow his or her spirit to dominate, taking charge to direct all emotions and behavior in obedience to Christ.

THE BODY

From the time of our salvation, we are fully His—spirit, soul, and body. No more clearly do we see this than in First Corinthians 6:19-20: "Or do you not know that your body is the temple of the Holy Spirit who is in you, whom you have from God, and you are not your own? For you were bought at a price; therefore glorify God in your body and in your spirit, which are God's." God has given us our "earth suit" to care for and not abuse by overworking, overeating, and underexercising. It is our reasonable service to present this same body to God as a living sacrifice acceptable and pleasing to Him (see Rom. 12:1).

Psychosomatic illnesses presently fill our hospitals; these are physical illnesses with the root cause being in the soul realm. This is no new revelation, as the Bible has always informed us of how inter-related all parts of our being are: "A sound heart is life to the body, but envy is rottenness to the bones" (Prov. 14:30). This is true for the other way around as well. Many times as I counsel people for problems in their soul, I understand that their physical ailments contribute massively to their defeated emotional condition. As they are physically fatigued, unhealthy, overweight, or on a lot of medication, their soul is weighed down and overwhelmed by the knock-on negative effect of their body.

Our moods, emotions, and self-esteem are directly affected and "infected" by the state of our physical bodies. Likewise, our sleep patterns, ability to get up in the morning, energy levels, stamina, and ability to handle stress are directly connected to our outward person. We may pray for miracles for God to refresh, energize, and heal our bodies, but this is not independent of us taking the ownership to exercise self-control over our physical bodies. Many people live with the consequences of an old, tired, or sickly body brought on by an undisciplined life because they expect God to do for them what He has instructed us to do for ourselves.

Repentance for eating a nutritionally-starved diet with too much junk food is our first point of call before we go to God for healing. We cannot expect God to look after the body He has given us charge over! Do not be deceived into thinking that such care of the physical body is vanity, for it is much more than that. Let us not allow the devil to send us to Heaven young and prematurely, short-circuiting our calling and destiny because we did not take care of the body God gave to us for safe-keeping.

At one time in my life, after having traveled extensively, preaching, ministering, counseling, and training others, I found myself spiritually and emotionally depleted. Before I could refresh or restore myself, the enemy came in like a flood and I could not withstand his attack. Consequently, I crashed and burned, and it took me several weeks to fully recover and revive my strength. One of my saving graces was my physical fitness and health, which gave me the stamina and strength to sustain me until the other areas of my life became restored. God has given us spirit, soul, and body to synergize together to accomplish His will here on earth.

THE SOUL

Picasso the painter said, "It takes a long time to become truly young, because youth know no age." We like to call the older group in our church the JOY group for "Just Older Youth" because we view youthfulness as an inward state of being rather than an outward chronological age. We have several "young" older people in our church who have not allowed themselves to be defined by the containment of their physical bodies. "Therefore we do not lose heart. Even though our outward man is perishing, yet the inward man is being renewed day by day" (2 Cor. 4:16). Christians, no matter what age, can be especially guilty of not having a youthful attitude about their lives and become very serious and boring about everything! We must learn to have fun and enjoy our lives if we are not already doing so.

Writer Agatha Christie joked, "An archaeologist is the best husband any woman can have: the older she gets, the more interested he is in her!" Becoming older can often mean we become a little too comfortable and complacent with the familiar and don't like changing our traditions. However, these traditions do not promote a youthful attitude, as we can end up resisting God and anything new that He is introducing into our lives. Change must always be part of our lives because it is part of God. The young are known to be much more flexible, but this is an inward attitude we do not have to lose as we grow older. We must always be prepared to risk something new and even a little intimidating. We could take a computer course, learn a new skill, do things differently, or return to previous hobbies or activities from our youth. It may feel unauthentic to start with, but persevere; we will never know if we are not prepared to try. Don't give in to old insecurities that try to make you back down, simply "Do it afraid!"

Mark Twain said, "Age is an issue of mind over matter. If you don't mind, it doesn't matter." If our self-worth and self-esteem are dependent on the outward person being young and attractive, we will struggle with the decaying of the natural body that the Bible talks about. However, if our goal is to gain wisdom and understanding, then time and aging are a gift. Growing physically older has many God-given blessings, and I personally love each year I grow older. "The glory of young men is their strength, and the splendor of old men is their gray head" (Prov. 20:29); the Amplified version of this Scripture suggests that a gray head refers to wisdom and experience. Getting older does not necessarily bring wisdom (we know that all old people are not wise), but rather wisdom must be searched for, understood, and applied with each passing year for it to become a precious treasure. Time proves that God is a reality, as we no longer theorize but experience His goodness: "I have been young, and now am old; yet I have not seen the righteous forsaken, nor his descendants begging bread" (Ps. 37:25).

The young have vigor and strength, and they naturally want to and should challenge the old, traditional ways that may no longer be relevant. Although the Gospel never changes, our methods of getting the Gospel out to our community should always be updated because our culture is always changing. God has blessed and enriched the Women In Touch team with every age group, and I have learned to value and appreciate all their input. At times, the youth carry more responsibilities than those double their age. Age will never disqualify anyone from being used of God:

> Then said I: "Ah, Lord God! Behold, I cannot speak, for I am a *youth*." But the Lord said to me: "Do not say, 'I am a *youth*,' for you shall go to all to whom I send you, and whatever I command you, you shall speak. Do not be afraid of their faces, for I am with you to deliver you," says the Lord (Jeremiah 1:6-8).

True youthfulness does not come with the arrogant or rebellious attitude that is sometimes synonymous with the young in age; not even they are excused from living an exemplary lifestyle. "Let no one despise your **youth,** but be an example to the believers in word, in conduct, in love, in spirit, in faith, in purity" (1 Tim. 4:12). They must come to appreciate and understand that they do not know everything, and that they place themselves in opposition with God when they react in ways that are prideful and arrogant. Many old traditions remain precious and valid and retain the touch of God. Let us stay humble and accept the wisdom from "older youth," lest God Himself humiliate us (see 1 Pet. 5:5).

THE SPIRIT

We are born again into the Kingdom of God as spiritual babes, and then we are required to grow up in Him and become mature. Our spiritual maturity, therefore, does not depend on chronological age, rather it depends on our determination to feed off the solid food of the Word of God. This will distinguish those who are thirty-year old spiritual babes with less maturity than those who have been walking with God for three years (see Heb. 5:12-14).

"The spirit of a man will sustain him in sickness, but who can bear a broken spirit?" (Prov. 18:14). Just as I needed to restore my strength that time, so it is vital that no matter what our chronological or spiritual age, we learn to refresh ourselves in the Lord to keep our youthfulness, spirit, soul, and body. All three parts of our being need to sustain us so we can finish our race strong. Psalm 103:5 tells us God is well able to renew our youth, but this does not come from passivity, empty thinking, or inactivity. We are to be diligent in obeying His Word, and we should:

- Allow God to lead us beside still waters so He can restore our souls (see Ps. 23:2).

- Feed and drink of God alone so He can satisfy the appetites of our human soul (see Isa. 51:1-2).

- Repent of our sin so that times of refreshing might come from His presence (see Acts 3:19).

- Discipline our mind on Him so that He can keep us in perfect peace (see Isa. 26:3).

- Pray in the Holy Spirit so we can build ourselves up (see Jude 20).

Have you not known? Have you not heard? The everlasting God, the Lord, the Creator of the ends of the earth, neither faints nor is weary. His understanding is unsearchable. He gives power to the weak, and to those who have no might He increases strength. Even the youths shall faint and be weary, and the young men shall utterly fall, but those who wait on the Lord shall renew their strength; they shall mount up with wings like eagles, they shall run and not be weary, they shall walk and not faint (Isaiah 40:28-31).

Chapter 26

Zeroing-In on Zest

In this final chapter, it is time to zero in on an aspect not yet covered. The definition of our word *zest* is "hearty enjoyment, gusto; anything added to impart flavor and enhance ones appreciation of; liveliness, energy or enthusiasm." To conclude our journey through *The ABC's of Relationships*, we must remember to always retain a gusto and zest, an enjoyment, enthusiasm, and energy for the process of growth that God called us to. We may not be where we want to be in our relationships, but we can thank God that we are also not where we used to be either! This is the cherry on top of our cake of relationship building; the zest we need to impart the flavor and spice to our lives, ensuring we appreciate all that He is doing in and through us. We also welcome all that we can give to and receive from our different relationships, secure in the knowledge that He is in control of our lives.

Ralph Waldo Emerson said, "Nothing great was ever achieved without enthusiasm."[1] Zest is the level of enthusiasm and excitement with which we do life. In Greek, *enthusiasm* means "God in us." We already have this enthusiasm because God is in us, and He will manifest His life through us with a zest for living and a positive excitement for all His ways. Enthusiasm makes the difference between enduring life's difficulties and enjoying life's journey. We're drawn in by the energy and passion that enthusiastic people have because enthusiastic people are energy-givers. Enthusiastic people inspire us to become more confident, help us be our best, and teach us to share ourselves more willingly with others. Henry David Thoreau said, "None are so old as those who have outlived enthusiasm."

Four Main Characteristics of Zest

The four main characteristics of zest are presence, passion, positive, and power. These four powerful P's are defined as:

> **Presence:** enthusiastic people will be thermostats, not thermometers, in a home, family, or church; they will set the level of excitement and energy around them rather than being determined by it or the lack of it.

> **Passion:** enthusiastic people will put their heart into anything they are involved in; they are upbeat, street-wise, have a "wow" in their speech, gusto in their style, and a dance in their step.

> **Positive:** enthusiastic people focus on what others want rather than on what they do not want; they focus on finding opportunities in every problem instead of problems in every opportunity.

> **Power:** enthusiastic people are self-confident and radiate a positive power to all those around them; it is an assurance of God's greatness and destiny within them.

Og Mandino said, "Every memorable act in the history of the world is a triumph of enthusiasm. Nothing great was ever achieved without it because it gives any challenge or any occupation, no matter how frightening or difficult, a new meaning. Without enthusiasm you are doomed to a life of mediocrity but with it you can accomplish miracles."[3]

Endnotes

1. http://www.quotationspage.com/quote/29687.html.

2. http://thinkexist.com/quotation/none_are_so_old_as_those_who_have_outlived/208120.html.

3. http://quotationsbook.com/quote/12584/.

Bibliography

———◆·◆·◆———

Bolton, Robert. *People Skills*. New York: Simon & Schuster, Inc; Touchstone, 1979.

Cloud, Henry and John Townsend. *Boundaries*. Grand Rapids, MI: Zondervan, 1992.

Covey, Steve. *The Seven Habits of Highly Successful People*. New York: Simon & Schuster, 1989.

Hayford, Jack. *Prayer is Invading the Impossible*. Alachua, FL: Bridge-Logos, 2002.

Henry, Matthew. *Matthew Henry's Commentary on the Whole Bible*. Peabody, MA: Hendrickson Publishers, Inc., 1991.

Jakes, T.D. *Maximize the Moment*. New York: G.B.Putnam's Sons, 1999.

Maxwell, John. *The Winning Attitude*. Nashville, TN: Thomas Nelson Publishers, 1993.

Maxwell, John. *The 17 Indisputable Laws of Teamwork*. Nashville, TN: Thomas Nelson Inc., 2001.

Murray, Andrew. *Humility*. Alachua, FL: Bridge-Logos Publishers, 2000.

Nichols, Ralph and Leonard Stevens. *Are you listening?* New York: McGraw-Hill, 1957.

Philips, Bob. *Controlling Your Emotions.* Eugene, OR: Harvest House Publishers, 1995

Powell, John. *The Secret of Staying in Love.* Kernersville, NC: Argus Communications, 1974.

Smalley, Gary. *The DNA of Relationships.* Colorado Springs, CO: Smalley Publishing Group, 2007.

About the Author

Marion Meyers is the founder of Women In Touch, an international women's ministry. A counselor for over 25 years, she is also part of a national revolutionary women's ministry, ministers at conferences, and supports local churches in their endeavors to pioneer and enrich their women's ministry. She and her husband co-pastor two churches in England where they live with their two adult children.

ANOTHER EXCITING TITLE BY MARION MEYERS

Somewhere between learning your ABC's and now, a lot has happened. Maybe you lost your job, your parents, your spouse, your sense of security—your temper. Armed with the Word of God and drawing on 25 years as a social worker and full-time minister, Marion Meyers battles a wide range of emotional topics and issues that attack people every day.

ISBN: 978-88-89127-32-2

Order now from Destiny Image Europe
Telephone: +39 085 4716623 - Fax: +39 085 9431270
E-mail: orders@eurodestinyimage.com
Internet: www.eurodestinyimage.com

Additional copies of this book and other book
titles from DESTINY IMAGE™ EUROPE
are available at your local bookstore.

We are adding new titles every month!

To view our complete catalog online, visit us at:
www.eurodestinyimage.com

Send a request for a catalog to:

Via Acquacorrente, 6
65123 - Pescara - ITALY
Tel. +39 085 4716623 - Fax +39 085 9431270

"Changing the world, one book at a time."

Are you an author?

Do you have a "today" God-given message?

CONTACT US

We will be happy to review your manuscript
for the possibility of publication:

publisher@eurodestinyimage.com
http://www.eurodestinyimage.com/pages/AuthorsAppForm.htm